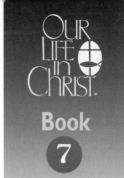

OUR LIFE in CHRIST.

Book 7

W9-CQQ-382

Adult
Bible Studies

By Thomas J. Doyle
and James R. Gimbel

CPH
SAINT LOUIS

Portions of the "Inform" and "Connect" sections were written by Ken Wagener.

This publication is available in braille and in large print for the visually impaired. Write to the Library for the Blind, 1333 S. Kirkwood Rd., St. Louis, MO 63122-7295, or call 1-800-433-3954.

Copyright © 1999, 2002 Concordia Publishing House
3558 South Jefferson Avenue, St. Louis, MO 63118-3968
Manufactured in the United States of America

4   5   6   7   8   9   10   11   12   13   11   10   09   08   07   06   05   04   03   02

Contents

Leaders Guide

Introduction

God promises to strengthen our life in Christ as we study His Word. The Our Life in Christ Bible study series provides you resources to help you study God's Word. The series gives you an opportunity for in-depth study of some familiar and, possibly, not-so-familiar Bible stories.

Each of the 9 Bible study books in this series has 13 sessions that are divided into 4 easy-to-use sections.

Focus—Section 1 of each session focuses the participant's attention on the key concept that will be discovered in the session.

Inform—Section 2 explores a portion of Scripture with a brief commentary and through discussion questions that help each participant study the text.

Connect—Section 3 helps the participants see God's Law and Gospel in the scriptural account and apply it to their lives.

Vision—Section 4 provides the participants with practical suggestions for applying the theme of the session in places other than the classroom and even in their families.

Our Life in Christ is designed to assist both novice and expert Bible students in their study of Holy Scripture. It offers resources that will enable them to grow in their understanding of God's Word while strengthening their life in Christ.

The sessions in this Our Life in Christ adult Bible study series follow the Scripture lessons taught in the Our Life in Christ Sunday school series. Parents will enjoy grappling with the same Bible stories their children are studying in Sunday school. This will provide parents and children additional opportunities to

- discuss God's Word together;
- extend session applications to everyday situations;
- pray together; and
- engage in family activities that grow out of the session truths.

We pray that as you study God's Word using the Our Life in Christ Bible study series, your life in Christ may be strengthened.

Adult Study Guide

God Provides
a Leader for His People

(1 Samuel 16:1–23; 2 Samuel 1:1–6:23)

Focus

Theme: God Chooses!

Law/Gospel Focus

All people disobey God's Law. By nature, all people stand guilty before God, as partners in the first rebellion against His Word in the Garden of Eden. But God in His love for us has chosen for us to receive the gift of forgiveness of sins and eternal life through faith in His Son Jesus' death on the cross. God's love empowers and motivates us to serve Him and others.

Objectives

By the power of the Holy Spirit working through God's Word, we will
1. describe the events leading up to and including David's anointing as king by Samuel;
2. explain why, when compared to his brothers, David seems an unlikely choice for king;
3. thank God for choosing us to be His servants, who because of sin deserve only His condemnation;
4. explain how God through our faith in Christ Jesus has equipped us with strength so that we may abound in good works.

Opening Worship

Read in unison Psalm 24.

The earth is the LORD's, and everything in it,

---

the world, and all who live in it;
for He founded it upon the seas
and established it upon the waters.
Who may ascend the hill of the LORD?
Who may stand in His holy place?
He who has clean hands and a pure heart,
who does not lift up his soul to an idol
or swear by what is false.
He will receive blessing from the LORD
and vindication from God his Savior.
Such is the generation of those who seek Him,
who seek Your face, O God of Jacob.
Lift up your heads, O you gates;
be lifted up, you ancient doors,
that the King of glory may come in.
Who is this King of glory?
The LORD strong and mighty,
the LORD mighty in battle.
Lift up your heads, O you gates;
lift them up, you ancient doors,
that the King of glory may come in.
Who is He, this King of glory?
The LORD Almighty—
He is the King of glory.

Introduction

1. What characteristics do you look for in a leader? List as many as possible.

2. The Lord said to Samuel, "Man looks at the outward appearance, but the Lord looks at the heart." What insight does God imply in these words to Samuel?

3. Why is it important to seek God's guidance when selecting a leader? How might you seek His guidance?

Inform

Read 1 Samuel 16:1–23 and skim 2 Samuel 1:1–6:23.

About the Text

"A man after God's heart." David, the youngest son of Jesse, towers over the kings of Israel as God's chosen servant—a capable, faithful ruler of God's own people. The story of his call to leadership, from his humble roots as a shepherd, begins with the Lord's command to the prophet Samuel.

Samuel mourns for Saul because the Lord has rejected Saul as king of Israel. Samuel understands the consequence of God's decision—both Saul and his family will be destroyed in a vain attempt to maintain their positions of authority. But God's purpose must be fulfilled. Samuel is sent on another mission: to anoint a new ruler for the people, who will carry out the vital work of defending the nation against its many enemies.

David does not become king by virtue of military and political successes. He becomes king by virtue of the Lord's choice, a choice made when David is yet a boy. This is the highlight of the story: God chooses the son who has apparently been considered too young even for participation in the religious ceremony. The Lord looks at the heart rather than at the superficial externals. In David, God sees more than a simple, wind-burned, unspoiled shepherd; He sees His servant and Israel's future king. The Spirit of the Lord leaps upon David, descending with the force of lightning. By this anointing with the Holy Spirit, he is not only chosen to be God's instrument for saving Israel as king; he is also placed in the continuing line of leaders of God's people, a line that will extend to the King of the end time (Isaiah 11:2), who is baptized by the same Spirit, and who, after His glorification, will give His Spirit to His people in the messianic age without measure.

There are dangers, however, in anointing a new king. Saul is a jealous and, at times, reckless and violent man. In order to preserve Samuel's life, God instructs the prophet to invite Jesse and his sons to offer a special sacrifice. God will then reveal the successor to the throne. Samuel expects the oldest or most rugged of the brothers to be chosen as king, but God has other plans. Samuel learns an important lesson about God's gracious call: "Man looks at the outward appearance, but the LORD looks at the heart" (1 Samuel 16:7). God shows no partiality; He alone chooses and provides the strength and resources for faithful service. Though seven of Jesse's sons pass before Samuel, God directs the prophet to David, the youngest, a shepherd. David appears before Samuel, and he anoints the young man as king.

Saul dies a tragic death—at the hands of the Philistines and a ruffian Amalekite. This sets the stage for David's anointing as king of both Israel and Judah. In the years ahead, David lives through civil war and frequent opposition from the supporters of Saul's family. Yet David's own power and reputation as a godly leader grow, as God guides His servant's life and reign to accomplish His purpose. Through David, God will establish the nation in its capital, Jerusalem. David's royal dynasty will lead to the future anointed king, the Messiah Jesus.

Discussing the Text

1. Why does God reject Saul as king?

2. What virtue does David possess that causes God to choose him as Saul's successor? Why is this significant?

3. Describe the events that lead to David's anointing as king? What important lesson does Samuel learn in the process?

4. What dangers does David face after Samuel anoints him as king? How does God demonstrate His control and preservation in these events?

Connect

"I have rejected [Saul] as king," God announces to Samuel (1 Samuel 16:1). By his words and actions, Saul has shown himself to be a faithless leader for the nation. He was once an "impressive young man without equal" (1 Samuel 9:2), called to deliver the people from the tyranny of the Philistines. Now he frequently disobeys the Word of the Lord. Once a man of faith and strength in the promise of God, he demonstrates contempt for God's ways. He seeks his own personal success and glory.

Like Saul, all people disobey God's righteous law. By nature, every human being stands guilty before God, a partner in the first rebellion against His Word in the Garden of Eden. Moreover, the deliberate choice to disregard God's will, to reject His ways for the broad path of selfish desire and honor, leads to God's pronouncement: "You [act] foolishly. … You have not kept the command the LORD your God gave you" (1 Samuel 13:13).

God chooses David by grace. It is not a matter of merit or past achievement, although David is a man of courage and skill (1 Samuel 17:34–35). Rather, God sends the prophet Samuel as a witness to His limitless mercy that redeems and equips His people to serve in His kingdom. David's humble status—youngest son and shepherd—is not a liability as the world believes but instead an avenue for God's glory. As St. Paul notes, "God chose the foolish things of the world to shame the wise; God chose the weak things of the world to shame the strong ... so that no one may boast before Him" (1 Corinthians 1:27, 29).

The Lord's promise is the true power behind the throne. As God guides, protects, and blesses his reign over the people, David expresses his thankfulness in his many psalms and in his just rule over God's people.

Today, God calls His people into His kingdom of mercy and love not on the basis of our goodness or merit but by His grace alone. The Lord Jesus chose us, St. Paul notes, before the foundation of the world. Through Baptism we have been set apart—forgiven and renewed—and anointed with the Holy Spirit for ministry in Christ's name. In Christ, we are equipped with God's strength so that in all things, at all times, we may abound in every good work (2 Corinthians 9:8).

1. What does Saul do that causes God to reject him as king? Where do you see evidence of similar behavior toward God today?

2. God chooses David to replace Saul. What makes David an unlikely candidate by human standards as Saul's replacement? What does God demonstrate to Israel in choosing David as king? What does God demonstrate by choosing David?

3. "But you are a chosen people, a royal priesthood, a holy nation, a people belonging to God, that you may declare the praises of Him who called you out of darkness into His wonderful light" (1 Peter 2:9). God chooses us to receive His gifts of forgiveness of sins and eternal life through faith in Jesus' death on the cross.

What makes us unlikely candidates for the positions of "a chosen people, a royal priesthood, a holy nation, a people belonging to God"? What does God demonstrate to us in choosing us to be heirs of the kingdom of heaven?

4. When God chooses us, He also equips us with His strength to do that which He desires. How do God's chosen people use the strength He gives by the power of the Holy Spirit to do that which He desires—"declare the praises of Him"? What do you demonstrate to others when you "declare the praises of Him who called you out of darkness into His wonderful light"?

Vision

To Do This Week

Family Connection

1. Review the story of the anointing of David to be king. Ask, "What makes God's choice so amazing?"

2. Get out memorabilia from your Baptism and the Baptism of other family members. Remind family members that God chose each of you at Baptism to be "a chosen people, a royal priesthood, a holy nation, a people belonging to God." Again ask, "What makes God's choice so amazing?" Emphasize that while you are sinners, God sent Jesus to suffer and to die on the cross for your sins. You receive forgiveness of sins and eternal life not because of anything you have done to deserve it but simply because of God's grace—undeserved love.

3. Consider how you might better demonstrate to others the fact that you are equipped by the Spirit's power to do good works.

Personal Reflection

1. Thank God for choosing you to be His heir to the kingdom of heaven through faith in Jesus.

2. Continue to see new ways by which God might equip you to serve Him. Remember the Holy Spirit works through God's Word to strengthen your faith, equipping you to serve Him.

Closing Worship

Sing or speak together the following stanzas of "Amazing Grace, How Sweet the Sound."

> Amazing grace! How sweet the sound
> That saved a wretch like me!
> I once was lost but now am found,
> Was blind but now I see!
>
> The Lord has promised good to me,
> His word my hope secures;
> He will my shield and portion be
> As long as life endures.
>
> Yes, when this flesh and heart shall fail
> And mortal life shall cease,
> Amazing grace shall then prevail
> In heaven's joy and peace.

For Next Week

Read 1 Samuel 17:55–20:42; 2 Samuel 5:1–5; 11:1–12:13; 14:25–18:33; and 22:1–51 in preparation for the next session.

Session 2

God Preserves David

(1 Samuel 17:55–20:42; 2 Samuel 5:1–5; 11:1–12:13;
14:25–18:33; 22:1–51)

Focus

Theme: Chosen, but Vulnerable

Law/Gospel Focus

Because of sin, we are vulnerable to attack by temptations from this world, Satan, and our own sinful self. Through His Word, God confronts our weakness and guilt and offers us His mercy and forgiveness through Jesus Christ. Through Jesus, God has purchased us from sin, death, and the power of Satan and promises us His eternal provision and care so that we can confess boldly with St. Paul, "[nothing] in all creation will be able to separate us from the love of God that is in Christ Jesus our Lord" (Romans 8:39).

Objectives

By the power of the Holy Spirit working through God's Word, we will
1. describe a few of the many struggles David faces in his life;
2. explain how God demonstrates His eternal care and provision in David's life;
3. share how God has demonstrated His eternal care and provision in our lives.

Opening Worship

Read in unison the words of Psalm 23.

The Lord is my shepherd, I shall not be in want.
    He makes me lie down in green pastures,
He leads me beside quiet waters,
    He restores my soul

He guides me in paths of righteousness
    for His name's sake.
Even though I walk
    through the valley of the shadow of death,
I will fear no evil,
    for You are with me;
Your rod and Your staff,
    they comfort me.
You prepare a table before me
    in the presence of my enemies.
You anoint my head with oil;
    my cup overflows.
Surely goodness and love will follow me
    all the days of my life,
and I will dwell in the house of the LORD forever.

Introduction

We confess that God has chosen us as His own through Jesus' blood shed on the cross. We also confess that we are vulnerable to be tempted by the world, by Satan, and by our own sinful self.

1. List evidence of how Christians are vulnerable to temptation.

2. Now confess silently your own vulnerability to temptation, evident in the sins you have committed.

3. Read aloud God's Word found in 1 John 1:9, "If we confess our sins, He is faithful and just and will forgive us our sins and purify us from all unrighteousness." What assurance do these words provide you?

In today's session we will examine the struggles, temptations, and sins of God's chosen servant David. Through all these experiences, God remains faithful to David and preserves, strengthens, and forgives him. God demonstrates the faithfulness shared with David to us in the person and work of Jesus Christ.

Inform

Read aloud 1 Samuel 17:55–20:42; 2 Samuel 5:1–5; 11:1–12:13; 14:25–18:33; and 22:1–51.

About the Text

Throughout his life David faces adversity, both from his enemies and from his own sinful desires. The readings in this text describe a few of his many struggles, as well as God's faithful supply and protection in the midst of these difficult situations.

Saul's attempts to kill David are prompted by jealousy and fear. The young man's victory over Goliath, the Philistine giant, secures his fame in Israel and cements his friendship with Jonathan, the king's son. Saul, in response, desires to turn a liability into a political triumph by promoting David within the army. With David's sworn allegiance to the king, Saul is able to watch over and control this new threat to his authority.

Yet jealousy and apprehension quickly evolve into fear. The celebration songs in praise of David provoke Saul to speculate on David's intention: "What more can he get but the kingdom?" (1 Samuel 18:8). When radical solutions fail, Saul proposes a marriage alliance to "shore up" their relationship. But David's success at love, leadership, and life in general is a clear sign to Saul: "The LORD was with David" (1 Samuel 18:28).

One highlight amidst David's troubles is his friendship with Jonathan. David trusts the crown prince, who reveals the king's designs to kill him. Even Jonathan's well-meant attempt at reassuring David does not allay his misgivings; in fact, David believes that the king has concealed his true intentions from his son because of his fear that Jonathan's great affection for David may upset the royal plan to kill him. Therefore, Jonathan's belief that he enjoys his father's confidence in all matters and will be able to warn David is an assumption that must be tested. The next day's festival of the new moon, David suggests, offers an excellent opportunity for a test that will expose Saul's intentions. David will use the sacred day as an excuse for absenting himself from the king's fellowship in order to attend the annual sacrificial meal of his kinsmen at Bethlehem; thus, he will allegedly put duty to his family before duty to his king. Saul's reaction will reveal whether or not David is in imminent danger. Jonathan agrees to this stratagem and assures David that he will under no circumstances betray the sacred covenant he has made with him.

The next day David's plan is put into effect. However, on that first day of the new-moon festival, his absence is passed over. The king imagines that some accident (such as contact with a dead body) has disqualified David from sharing in the royal meal, which has a religious significance and therefore requires ritual preparation. It is only on the second day that Saul's intentions are clearly revealed. David's explanation for his absence, which Jonathan now repeats, is most skillful. Kinship obligations were among the most pressing and urgent duties of that day; indeed, David's obligation to his kin and their covenant with the Lord supersedes his obligation to Saul. The king, however, does not acknowledge this. When Jonathan excuses David on the ground that his duty to kinsmen takes precedence, Saul breaks out in anger, practically disowning Jonathan as an illegitimate bastard who is unworthy of his high birth. Saul claims that it is rebellion for Jonathan to prefer any covenant bond with David to what should be his undivided duty toward the royal family.

Jonathan now suffers affliction out of his loyalty to his covenant of love with David. He remains loyal to David even when it brings him into conflict with his father and costs him the kingship. God uses Jonathan's abiding friendship with David to preserve the future king's life.

Indeed, God richly blesses David. The Lord protects His servant through numerous plots against his life, through civil war and rebellion in his own family, and through frequent battles with foreign nations. God also "preserves" David from judgment and punishment when he transgresses the divine law. David's verdict on Nathan's parable, "The man who did this deserves to die!," is a statement of self-condemnation. Yet the prophet speaks God's Word of forgiveness as the king cries out, "I have sinned against the LORD" (2 Samuel 12:13).

Discussing the Text

1. What adversities does David face?

2. What prompts Saul's desire to harm David?

3. How does God use the friendship between David and Jonathan to preserve David's life?

4. What events demonstrate the depth of Jonathan's love for David?

5. How is the Lord's protection and preservation evident in the life of David?

Connect

David is God's servant, chosen by grace and strengthened by the Lord's almighty power. David is also a mortal man, vulnerable before earthly kings and armies. At times he capitulates to his sinful passions. He deserves God's punishment. In his many psalms, he admits his absolute dependence on God for protection: "See how my enemies have increased and how fiercely they hate me! Guard my life and rescue me; let me not be put to shame, for I take refuge in You" (Psalm 25:19–20). Above all, though, David needs God's forgiveness: "I said, 'O LORD, have mercy on me; heal me, for I have sinned against You' " (Psalm 41:4). God, through His Word and His prophets, confronts David with the reality of his weakness and guilt.

God preserves David because of His love in Christ, David's son and Lord. The Gospel is the love of the heavenly Father toward His wandering children, love that searches for, finds, saves, and protects the lost. Martin Luther writes, "We confess that God the Father not only has given us all that we have and see before our eyes, but also daily guards and defends us against every evil and misfortune, warding off all sorts of danger and disaster. All this He does out of pure love and goodness, without our merit, as a kind father who cares for us so that no evil may befall us" (*Large Catechism*, the Creed, 17). In Jesus, God our Father has redeemed His people and has promised us His eternal provision and care. Nothing in all creation shall ever separate us from His love in Christ our Lord (Romans 8:39).

1. Why is there danger in making David the hero of the story? Who is the real hero?

2. God is the hero in our story, too. Tell how God has demonstrated His love for you in spite of your sin.

3. Add your own words to the words of Martin Luther. After the phrase "all that we have and see before our eyes," list the blessings God has given you. After the phrase "daily guards and defends us against every evil and misfortune," list ways that God has demonstrated this in your life. Prepare to share your words along with Martin Luther's words during the "Closing Worship" activity.

Vision

To Do This Week

Family Connection

1. Give each family member a blank sheet of paper. Ask, "What dangers did David face in his life?" Direct each person to draw a picture showing a danger David faced. Ask, "How did God protect David?"

2. Next give each family member another blank sheet of paper. Ask, "What dangers or troubles have we faced in life?" Again, direct each person to draw a picture. Ask, "How has God protected us?"

3. Discuss the concept "hero." Ask, "Who are some heroes?" Then ask, "How is God always the ultimate hero?"

4. Design a family banner entitled "God is the [family name] family's hero."

Personal Reflection

1. Review Martin Luther's words. Meditate on how God has blessed, guarded, and defended you.

2. Pray that God will provide you the opportunity this week to share His love with someone who has faced or is facing hardships and troubles.

Closing Worship

Sing or speak together the following stanzas of "Have No Fear, Little Flock."

> Have no fear, little flock;
> Have no fear, little flock,
> For the Father has chosen
> To give you the Kingdom;
> Have no fear, little flock!
>
> Praise the Lord high above;
> Praise the Lord high above,
> For He stoops down to heal you,
> Uplift and restore you;
> Praise the Lord high above!
>
> Thankful hearts raise to God;
> Thankful hearts raise to God,
> For He stays close beside you,
> In all things works with you;
> Thankful hearts raise to God!

For Next Week

Read 2 Samuel 9:1–13 in preparation for the next session.

Session 3

David Shows Kindness to Mephibosheth

(2 Samuel 9:1–13)

Focus

Theme: In Response to God's Love

Law/Gospel Focus

Because of our sin, we deserve nothing but God's wrath. But God in His love sent Jesus to live a perfect life on our behalf and suffer and die on the cross for our sins so that He might bestow on us the gift of forgiveness of sins and eternal life. His undeserved love for us empowers us to demonstrate undeserved love for others.

Objectives

By the power of the Holy Spirit working through God's Word, we will
1. describe the motivation for the love David demonstrates to Mephibosheth;
2. confess the depth of God's love for us, demonstrated in the person and work of Jesus;
3. demonstrate undeserved love to others.

Opening Worship

Read in unison the confession of faith found in Philippians 2:6–11.

> Who, being in very nature God,
>   did not consider equality with God something to be
>   grasped,
> but made Himself nothing,
>   taking the very nature of a servant,

being made in human likeness.
And being found in appearance as a man,
   He humbled Himself
   and became obedient to death—
     even death on a cross!
Therefore God exalted Him to the highest place
   and gave Him the name that is above every name,
that at the name of Jesus every knee should bow,
   in heaven and on earth and under the earth,
and every tongue confess that Jesus Christ is Lord,
   to the glory of God the Father.

Introduction

A favorite Christian song ends each refrain with the words "And they'll know we are Christians by our love."

1. How do people you meet know or find out that you are Christian?

2. Read Jesus' words from Luke 6:27–36. What challenge do you find in these words?

3. Now compare the words of Jesus in Luke 6 to St. Paul's words in Romans 5:6–11.

4. God loves us although we are His enemies because of sin. What opportunities might He provide for us to love our enemies?

In today's session David demonstrates love to someone who has done nothing to deserve his love. In so doing, David has the opportunity and privilege to demonstrate the enormity of God's love for him.

Inform

Read 2 Samuel 9:1–13.

About the Text

Saul's family has experienced much heartache and tragedy. David's desire, prompted by God's goodness to him, is to "show kindness" in tribute to Jonathan.

Saul's faithful servant, Ziba, seems to expect the worst from the king's summons. His replies to the king's questions are curt. He emphasizes that the sole survivor of Saul's house is lame and therefore certainly cannot cause the king any harm. Through this servant, David contacts Mephibosheth, who is hiding out with a Trans-Jordanian sheikh (in the very region where Ishbosheth had once set up his rival kingdom).

Mephibosheth comes to his command audience with the king filled with great anxiety. David, however, bids him dismiss his fears and reveals his real reason for summoning him: the steadfast love or covenant-loyalty he is obligated to show to his friend Jonathan's house. As concrete proof of his good intentions, David grants Mephibosheth all the crown land of his house, land that has fallen into David's royal possession. David's personal invitation that Mephibosheth live at the court is, however, more than a mere honor; it enables David to keep an eye on Saul's grandson and to counter any traitorous plans that might develop. Mephibosheth obeys and comes to live in Jerusalem.

The management of Saul's former royal estate is delegated by David to the servant Ziba, who has the necessary family and servants to farm the land and provide sufficient revenue to support his master's household at the capital. For the rest of his life, Mephibosheth has a privileged status at court ("like one of the king's sons").

Near the end of his life, David recognizes the need to provide for a peaceful transfer of power to his appointed successor. Adonijah, David's oldest son, takes the initiative without David's blessing and attempts to seize the throne with the support of various court officials at a feast. Yet the prophet Nathan, who once confronted the king about his sins of adultery and murder, intervenes to warn Bathsheba and, by extension, David.

When Bathsheba and Nathan together inquire into the king's plan for a successor, David acts decisively. He names Solomon, Bathsheba's son, as ruler, and orders the young man to be brought to Gihon for a formal presentation and anointing. As news of the decision arrives at Adonijah's feast, his supporters and guests quickly flee, and Adonijah seeks asylum in God's house. Solomon is now the undisputed king of Israel.

The incidents in 1 Chronicles 28–29 and 1 Kings 3 reveal the grace of God in the lives of His servants David and Solomon. David convenes a solemn religious assembly to convey to his son the great responsibility for building the temple. He appeals to the people in general, but to Solomon in particular, to acknowledge God, to follow His commands, and to serve Him faithfully through all generations.

David's final words to the nation are a magnificent prayer of praise, humble confession, and confident trust in the promise of God. He concludes his lengthy petition by asking God's blessing upon His people and upon Solomon, who now inherits the task of building God's house.

David's prayer for faithfulness and obedience for his son are fulfilled during the early years of Solomon's reign. Shortly after assuming the kingship, Solomon declares a period of festival days and sacrifices at Gibeon, the site of the Tent of Meeting and an important place of worship for Israel. There God appears to the new king with a gracious invitation: "Ask for whatever you want Me to give you" (2 Chronicles 1:7). Solomon responds in faith and humility. Like his father David, Solomon acknowledges God's generous gifts, yet also confesses his heartfelt need as he undertakes to rule God's people.

Pleased by Solomon's request, the Lord promises not only wisdom but wealth and honor too. God calls Solomon to a life of faith and submission to His will. By God's blessing, and under Solomon's leadership, Israel will rise to new heights of splendor. The temple, the dwelling of God among humankind, is now ready to be built as a place of worship for Israel and all nations (1 Kings 8).

Discussing the Text

1. Why had Saul's family experienced much tragedy?

2. What prompts David's desire to "show kindness" to Saul's family?

3. How does David demonstrate undeserved love to Mephibosheth?

4. What does Mephibosheth's "privileged status" mean?

Connect

David and Solomon understand their need before God. They lack true knowledge of His will; they lack the inner strength to assume the responsibility of leading God's people. Both kings require the guidance and resolve that God alone gives. God's kindness to His people is always rooted in and focused on His love in Christ. The Good News of forgiveness dispels the threat of judgment under the Law and banishes the fear and shame God's people feel over their sinfulness. In His ministry Jesus often speaks these simple words, "Take heart ... your sins are forgiven" (Matthew 9:2; Luke 7:48). The Gospel is God's compassion in full display. Our loving Father, who sent His Son into the world to redeem His children from bondage to sin and death, welcomes us home and into His warm embrace. It is the Father's will that "everyone who looks to the Son and believes in Him shall have eternal life" (John 6:40). In Christ's death and resurrection we witness the depth and height, the power and purposefulness, of God's kindness toward His creation.

God's people respond to His love by sharing their forgiveness with others. David's concern for the kingdom flows from his experience of God's goodness, and together with his son, Solomon, David desires to honor God by wisely serving God's people. United with Christ in Baptism, joined together with one another in His body and blood, God's people today offer their lives in response to His salvation. We are a family brought from death to life to serve our brothers and sisters and everyone whom the Lord desires to call into His body, the church.

1. Provide evidence that families today still experience tragedy and heartache. What is the cause of this heartache?

2. What prompts God to show kindness to all families? How does God demonstrate undeserved love to all people? See Romans 5:6–11.

3. We, too, have received privileges before God through faith in Christ Jesus. Read about our privileged status in 1 Peter 2:9–10. What does this status mean?

4. God's love and forgiveness for David motivate him to love others. How can we and do we demonstrate God's love for us to others?

Vision

To Do This Week

Family Connection

1. Review the events of 2 Samuel 9:1–13.

2. Remind family members that Mephibosheth does nothing to deserve David's love.

3. Say, "We were born sinners, separated from God and His love. But God in His love for us sent His only Son Jesus to suffer and to die on the cross for our sins. What did we do to deserve the forgiveness of sins and eternal life that Jesus won for us on the cross?" After a few moments, emphasize that we did nothing to earn or deserve God's love.

4. Say or write the words, "We love others as God first loved us." Have family members describe how God's love in Christ Jesus motivates us to love others.

Personal Reflection

1. Confess your sins to God.

2. Give thanks for the depth of God's love revealed in the person and work of Jesus.

3. Pray that the Holy Spirit will empower you to love others as God first loved you.

Closing Worship

Sing or speak together the first stanza of "Love Divine, All Love Excelling."

> Love divine, all love excelling,
> Joy of heav'n, to earth come down!
> Fix in us Thy humble dwelling,
> All Thy faithful mercies crown.
> Jesus, Thou art all compassion,
> Pure, unbounded love Thou art;
> Visit us with Thy salvation,
> Enter ev'ry trembling heart.

For Next Week

Read 1 Kings 5:1–8:66 in preparation for the next session.

Session 4

Solomon Builds the Temple

(1 Kings 5:1–8:66)

Focus

Theme: House of Worship—Our Congregation

Law/Gospel Focus

Our sin separated us from God and His presence. But God came to us in the person of Jesus Christ, who "became flesh and made His dwelling among us" to take upon Himself the sins of the world and die on the cross for those sins so that we might live eternally in God's presence. He continues to dwell among us in our houses of worship—our "congregations"—in His Word and Sacraments, through which His Spirit works to nurture our faith and empower us for Christian living.

Objectives

By the power of the Holy Spirit working through God's Word, we will
1. describe the building of the temple by Solomon;
2. summarize the events that took place on the day of dedication;
3. explain the means by which God dwells among us today;
4. compare the Christian congregation to the house of worship.

Opening Worship

Read in unison the words of Psalm 119:105–112.

> Your word is a lamp to my feet
>   and a light for my path.
> I have taken an oath and confirmed it,
>   that I will follow Your righteous laws.

I have suffered much;
    preserve my life, O LORD, according to Your word.
Accept, O LORD, the willing praise of my mouth,
    and teach me Your laws.
Though I constantly take my life in my hands,
    I will not forget Your law.
The wicked have set a snare for me,
    but I have not strayed from Your precepts.
Your statues are my heritage forever;
    they are the joy of my heart.
My heart is set on keeping Your decrees
    to the very end.

Introduction

Two advertisements for local congregations are printed side-by-side in a religion supplement of a newspaper.

One ad reads

Worship in a beautiful setting this Sunday! Experience the comfort of padded pews. Enjoy music played from our new 50-rank pipe organ. Marvel at the brilliant color of radiant cut glass. Fresh flowers and live plants adorn the marble altar. Experience worship as it was meant to be experienced!

The other ad reads

Hear God's Word proclaimed! Marvel at God's love for all people—revealed in the person and work of Jesus Christ. Enjoy the fellowship of believers who confess together their sin, receive the assurance of God's forgiveness in Christ Jesus, and, by the power of the Holy Spirit working through Word and Sacrament, share His love with each other.

1. Compare the two advertisements.

2. Which of these advertisements best describes a church?

3. Why might some people be inclined to select the church with the padded pews rather than the church where people confess their sins?

In today's session we learn about the building and dedication of the temple in Jerusalem by Solomon. We will discover that which is most important in a church—not the building and its appointments, but what goes on within its walls.

Inform

Read 1 Kings 5:1–8:66.

About the Text

The building of the temple, by God's direction, provides a central place for the people of God to gather in worship and prayer. After years of relying on a portable structure and various sites set apart for sacrifices, Israel now experiences the presence of God in a permanent location. In a stirring display of His glory and power, God comes to His temple to dwell among His people.

As Solomon prepares for the project, he looks first to strengthen his relationship with Hiram, king of Tyre. The city/state is situated on the Mediterranean coast and is known for purple dye and cedar wood. David had established a firm friendship with Hiram, and Hiram rejoices to continue the alliance with David's wise son.

Solomon makes arrangements to purchase from Tyre large quantities of cedar and pine timber, in exchange for Israel's wheat and olive oil. Solomon also arranges for laborers from all the tribes and regions of Israel to contribute to the construction of the temple. (Resentment toward the forced labor policy is a factor in the later division of the kingdom.)

The basic building, on which construction begins 480 years after the exodus from Egypt, is 90 feet long by 30 feet wide by 45 feet high. The larger section, the Holy Place, leads to the Most Holy Place, the site of the annual sacrifice by the high priest. Along the front of the temple is a porch, and on every side are small chambers, three tiers high, designed as storerooms. The interior is lined with cedar and overlaid with gold. Of all the intricate details, perhaps the most significant is the pair of golden cherubim, symbols of God's guardians of the ark of the covenant. After seven years of work, the temple of God is dedicated by Solomon before the Israelite assembly. The sequence of events described below conveys the grandeur of the day of dedication.

1. The ark is brought up from a specific area in the southeastern part of Jerusalem, the city of David, and placed in the Most Holy Place under the wings of the cherubim. As the priests depart from the sanctuary, the temple is filled with the shekinah, the cloud of the Lord's presence.

2. Solomon serves as a priest-king, signifying his role as the Lord's anointed servant. As Solomon blesses the people, he recounts the nation's history and the fulfillment of God's ancient promises.

3. Solomon stands before the great bronze altar—located in the courtyard in front of the temple—and prays his dedicatory prayer, praising God's majesty and asking God to hear the petitions of His chosen people.

4. Solomon again blesses the assembly, invoking God's promise to be present and to guide and strengthen His people as they serve the Lord.

5. The final part of the dedication rite consists of sacrifices and daily celebrations over a two-week period.

Discussing the Text

1. What is God's purpose for the temple?

2. How is God's direction evident in the building of the temple? In its dedication?

3. Although much of the emphasis of today's assigned Scripture is on the materials used to build the temple and its features, clearly there is a different emphasis in the description of the dedication. What is the focus of the dedication? Why is this significant?

Connect

God appoints Solomon to build the temple, not David, his father (the latter had been a warrior who killed many men; see 1 Chronicles 28:3). As the focal point of community worship, the temple and priests play an important role in communicating God's Word to the nation. Above all, though, the temple is the place where sacrifices are made—sacrifices for the sins of the people.

The different types of offerings reflect an awareness of both God's righteousness and human sinfulness. No mortal can stand before God apart from God's forgiveness: the temple, the dwelling of God, is the appointed place where mercy is proclaimed and grace is granted to all who believe.

The temple is a sign of God's gracious presence among His people. For centuries, the Israelites looked forward to a permanent home, a prosperous, peaceful land in fulfillment of the Lord's ancient promises. The building of the temple is the culmination of their confidence and hope in the Word of the redeemer God.

Yet the temple and the worship rituals of the Old Testament are a prelude to God's full revelation in Christ. The divine presence—the cloud—that fills the sanctuary at the dedication service is surpassed by the divine presence in person—the incarnation in Jesus. "The Word became flesh," St. John writes, "and made His dwelling among us" (John 1:14). The glory of God is fully and decisively seen in the birth of the world's Savior, the only Son of God. Jesus is the true Temple of God, the Lord who comes to His own and takes upon Himself the sins of humankind.

God comes to His people through His chosen means, often with a tangible element. The Gospel Word is proclaimed in the preaching and teaching of the prophetic and apostolic message of the Holy Scriptures. Yet God also speaks through His visible Word—Baptism and the Lord's Supper—and bestows faith and blessing to His people through these Gospel gifts. As we gather weekly for worship, God meets us with Word and Sacrament, and we, His chosen people, receive His blessings with praise and thanksgiving. Our house of worship, our "congregation," is God's holy house, where His Spirit works to nurture our faith and to empower us for faithful Christian living. Individually, too, we are God's temple, the dwelling place of His Spirit (1 Corinthians 3:16–17; 6:19; Ephesians 2:22). At the end of time, in the splendor of heaven, the saints will live in the peace and joy of God and the Lamb, the eternal temple (Revelation 21:3, 22).

1. Some churches today are magnificent structures. Others are simple in architecture and appointments. What is more important than what a church looks like?

2. God comes to the people of Israel in the form of a cloud. How is God's presence in the cloud surpassed in Jesus?

3. How is God present today for His people? How does this presence emphasize the importance of what is done in a church rather than what a church looks like?

Vision

To Do This Week

Family Connection

1. Make a family collage with the title "Our Church."
2. Talk to your family about the importance of what goes on in your church during worship and Bible study.
3. Invite friends or loved ones to your church.

Personal Reflection

1. Thank God for His continued presence in the Word and Sacraments.

2. Consider new opportunities to use your gifts in service to your congregation.

3. Commend your pastor this week for continuing to share the Gospel in its truth and purity.

Closing Worship

Sing or speak together the first two stanzas of "God Himself Is Present."

> God Himself is present;
> Let us now adore Him
> And with awe appear before Him.
> God is in His temple;
> All within keep silence,
> Prostrate lie with deepest rev'rence.
> Him alone God we own,
> Him, our God and Savior;
> Praise His name forever!
>
> God Himself is present;
> Hear the harps resounding;
> See the hosts the throne surrounding!
> "Holy, holy, holy!"
> Hear the hymn ascending,
> Songs of saints and angels blending.
> Bow Your ear
> To us here:
> Hear, O Christ, the praises
> That Your Church now raises.

For Next Week

Read 1 Kings 17:1–19:18 and 2 Kings 1:1–2:18 in preparation for the next session.

Session 5

Elijah Goes to Heaven

(1 Kings 17:1–19:18; 2 Kings 1:1–2:18)

— Focus —

Theme: Hope in the Midst of Hardship

Law/Gospel Focus

Because of sin in this world we will experience hardships. We may at times be inclined to question God and doubt His control. God provides forgiveness for our lack of faith, and through His Word strengthens our faith in Jesus with the assurance of His presence at all times, in all situations, and in all places.

Objectives

By the power of the Holy Spirit working through God's Word, we will
1. describe the message from God that Elijah relays;
2. explain how God demonstrates His control and His presence in events experienced by Elijah;
3. confess that we often lack faith as we experience hardships and receive the assurance of God's forgiveness in Christ;
4. affirm God's presence in our lives at all times, in all places, and in all situations.

Opening Worship

Sing or speak together "Have No Fear, Little Flock."

Have no fear, little flock;
Have no fear, little flock,
For the Father has chosen
To give you the Kingdom;
Have no fear, little flock!

Have good cheer, little flock;
Have good cheer, little flock;
For the Father will keep you
In His love forever;
Have good cheer, little flock!

Praise the Lord high above;
Praise the Lord high above,
For He stoops down to heal you,
Uplift and restore you;
Praise the Lord high above!

Thankful hearts raise to God;
Thankful hearts raise to God,
For He stays close beside you,
In all things works with you;
Thankful hearts raise to God!

Introduction

At times we all experience hardships.

1. Describe a hardship recently experienced by you or someone you know.

2. How did you or the other person respond to the hardship?

3. How can hardships cause a person to question or doubt God's presence?

4. How can God use a hardship to draw people closer to Him?

5. Read Jesus' invitation to those experiencing hardships in Matthew 11:28–30. What hope does Jesus' invitation provide in the midst of hardships?

In today's session we read about the hardships faced by the people of Israel because of their sin and the sin of their leaders. God in His love and mercy provides a prophet to speak words of judgment so that the people will turn from their sin and once again confess God as their Lord. In the midst of hardship, God continues to demonstrate His presence and His care to those who remain faithful to Him.

Inform

Read 1 Kings 17:1–19:18 and 2 Kings 1:1–2:18.

About the Text

After Solomon's death, the kingdom of Israel is fractured by hostility and rebellion into two nations. The northern tribes, often called Israel, refuse to acknowledge Solomon's son, Rehoboam, as ruler. Jeroboam, son of a prominent official in Solomon's court, assumes the kingship of Israel, while Rehoboam serves as king of Judah, the Southern Kingdom.

Around 875 B.C., almost 100 years after Solomon began his reign over Israel, God calls Elijah to speak His Word to Ahab, king of the northern tribes. Elijah comes from a small village, Tishbe, but is sent by God on a monumental task: to call the nation to repentance. As God's servant, a chosen vessel to bring His message of judgment, Elijah confronts the high and mighty with striking courage and conviction. The meaning of his name—"The Lord is my God"—reveals his singular purpose: to return his fellow Israelites to faith in God and obedience to His will.

Elijah announces God's punishment upon the land: no dew or rain in the years ahead, except at the prophet's command. The drought, intended to call the people to repent of their idolatry and disobedience, creates a serious hardship for many, including a poor widow in a nearby region. God directs Elijah to Zarephath of Sidon, a country known for Baal worship, to receive his daily provision from this widow. God will use the drought and famine to demonstrate His power and grace for His people.

Though the situation seems grave, Elijah speaks and acts on the authority of the living God, whose goodness overflows in the midst of poverty and despair. God supplies flour and oil for the prophet, the widow, and her family. Elijah also raises the woman's son from death (1 Kings 17:17–24).

Some time afterward, Elijah presents Ahab and the prophets of Baal with a challenge: Let the true God reveal His glory and power. Baal is nothing more than an idol, Elijah knows, a sham made by sinful human beings in their own image. When the false prophets are unable to "awaken" their god, Elijah calls on the Lord, the God of Abraham, Isaac, and Israel, to consume the altar and the sacrificial animal. God answers in divine majesty. The people acknowledge that the Lord is God. The prophets are put to death.

Years later, God again calls Elijah to speak His word of judgment to Ahab's family. Ahaziah, successor to Ahab, has sent a delegation to the priests of Baal-Zebub to inquire about his health and future. Elijah rebukes the king and pronounces the Lord's verdict: "You will certainly die!"

The stories illustrate the conflict between Elijah, God's prophet, and the wicked kings of Israel. Against severe opposition, Elijah remains strong in faith and in his devotion to God's call. He is a true servant, ready to risk his own safety and comfort to bring God's Word of judgment to sinful humanity.

Elisha (a name that means "God is salvation"), Elijah's faithful companion and disciple for about eight years, accompanies the prophet on his final journey. Elijah's humility and regard for the young man likely move him to want to be alone when the Lord takes him to heaven in a whirlwind. Though he admonishes Elisha to remain behind, Elisha refuses to leave his master and mentor alone.

"The company of the prophets" are individuals who travel with and study under the great prophets. (Groups of prophets are located at Jericho, Bethel, and Gilgal; they will become Elisha's responsibility after Elijah's departure.) The Lord has revealed to the students at Bethel and Jericho what will happen to Elijah.

A "double portion" is the right of the firstborn (Deuteronomy 21:17), and Elisha is Elijah's firstborn spiritual son. In the tradition of his master, Elisha wants to accomplish great things for the Lord, more than any other prophet. Only God can answer such a request, however, and Elijah calls upon God to openly confirm or deny Elisha's special "allotment" with a sign.

Elijah is taken away to the glories of heaven by a fiery chariot and horses—a brilliant escort, in many respects beyond human understanding. "Chariots and horseman of Israel" may refer to Elijah himself. As an army of chariots and soldiers protects a country, so Elijah's presence and ministry offer a powerful protection against the enemies of Israel. Elisha expresses his deep grief and pain at the loss of his father in the faith by tearing his clothes.

"Where now is the LORD, the God of Elijah?" In asking this question, Elisha inquires whether the Lord has commissioned him to take Elijah's place. The Lord answers by dividing the Jordan River, as He had for Elijah. The students, recognizing the power of God, accept Elisha as their new spiritual leader and father.

Discussing the Text

1. What words of judgment does Elijah pronounce against the wicked kings of Israel?

2. How does God demonstrate compassion to the widow of Zarephath?

3. How does the Lord demonstrate judgment on Ahaziah for consulting the prophets of Baal (2 Kings 1:1–18)?

4. In what miraculous way is Elijah taken to heaven? How is this a sign to Elisha?

Connect

Elijah's ministry to the widow of Zarephath paints a vivid picture of the frailty and burden of human life. The woman's final act—to prepare a meal and die—conveys her hopelessness in a sinful world. Apart from God's miraculous provision, she has nothing to look forward to and no resources to survive the day.

Likewise, Ahaziah's idolatry and flagrant disregard for God's Word reveal the depths of human sinfulness, as the Lord's anointed king seeks the counsel and blessing of a foreign god. Ahaziah's heart is rebellious; he utterly rejects God's call and claim upon his life. He casts aside the divine Word of promise for empty assurances from the "lord of the flies" (Baal-Zebub). God's judgment against the king, spoken through His prophet Elijah, is just and fully deserved: "You will certainly die." Disobedience to God's will always brings condemnation and death.

Yet the Lord does not withhold His mercy from sinful human beings. The prophet Ezekiel proclaims God's gracious will: "I take no pleasure in the death of the wicked, but rather that they turn from their ways and live. Turn!" (Ezekiel 33:11). God desires that all people be saved; He calls His people to repent and to believe the Good News of forgiveness and life through His Son. The Gospel is God's provision for hopelessness and despair. Jesus' death and resurrection are the remedy for sin and eternal separation. Through Christ, God redeems the world from the curse of the Law and from idolatry and rebellion.

We are God's people, dearly loved and blameless in His sight. Yet we often appear more like the hopeless widow or the rebellious king than like strong, faithful Elijah and Elisha. Our personal mission in Christ's name is challenged by hardship, temptation, and direct opposition. The Spirit of God has promised to guide and support us as we seek to follow Christ and serve His people in the world. Jesus promises His disciples, "You will receive power when the Holy Spirit comes upon you; and you will be My witnesses" (Acts 1:8). Like the ancient prophets, God's people today are sealed with the Spirit at Holy Baptism, renewed daily and weekly through Word and Sacrament, and brought to fullness in Christ by His grace.

1. How does the Lord's provision to the widow give us hope and comfort as we face the burdens of this life?

2. How is God's judgment spoken by Elijah to Ahaziah, "You will certainly die," also appropriate for us to hear as sinners?

3. God does not withhold His mercy from sinners. Instead God desires that all people be saved. How is the Gospel—the Good News of Jesus' death on the cross for all sins—provision against the hopelessness and helplessness of sin?

4. Just before Jesus was taken up into heaven He spoke the words, "You will receive power when the Holy Spirit comes upon you; and you will be My witnesses" (Acts 1:8). How do these words provide you comfort and hope as you face troubles and hardships in this life? How do they direct us to live our lives?

Vision

To Do This Week

Family Connection

1. Review the ways in which God preserves and blesses His people as they face hardships. Ask, "How has God blessed and preserved us?"

2. Review the challenge made by Elijah to the prophets of Baal. How does God demonstrate His control? Someone has said that

anything or anyone that becomes number one in our lives rather than God is an idol. What are some idols that people have today? How are these idols as dangerous as the false god Baal? What does God provide to enable us to withstand the temptation to worship other gods? Remind family members that God continues to work today through His Word to strengthen our faith so that we can withstand the temptation to make things and people gods.

3. Draw a picture depicting Elijah being taken away to heaven. Label the picture "Jesus will take me to heaven too."

Personal Reflection

1. Confess your sin—the sin that caused God to send His only Son Jesus to suffer and die on the cross.

2. Praise God for the love He has revealed to you in the person and work of Jesus.

3. Consider how you might better witness God's love in Jesus to others.

Closing Worship

Sing or speak together the first stanza of "On Christ's Ascension I Now Build."

> On Christ's ascension I now build
> The hope of my ascension;
> This hope alone has always stilled
> All doubt and apprehension;
> For where the head is, there as well
> I know His members are to dwell
> When Christ will come and call them.

For Next Week

Read 2 Kings 5:1–19 in preparation for the next session.

Session 6

God Heals Naaman

(2 Kings 5:1–19)

Focus

Theme: God's Ways vs. Human Expectations

Law/Gospel Focus

Our sin dooms us to eternal damnation—separation from God. But God in His love for us has devised a plan for our rescue—a plan that could never be conceived by humans. God sent His only Son into this world to live a perfect life on our behalf and then suffer the punishment we deserve—death on the cross. We receive the gift of forgiveness of sins and eternal life not through any merit of our own, but instead simply as an undeserved gift of God through faith in Jesus. The means for healing the sin-sickness that dooms us to death is "foolishness" to those who continue to perish. We confess through faith that God's ways do not always follow human expectations, but through the "foolishness" of the cross God accomplishes His plan of salvation.

Objectives

By the power of the Holy Spirit working through God's Word, we will

1. summarize the events in the account of the healing of Namaan and how God's prescription for healing is received by others;
2. describe how God uses the slave girl to accomplish His will and purpose;
3. confess the means through which God provides us healing from sin-sickness;
4. share with others that which is beyond human comprehension—God became one of us in the person of Jesus and then suffered and died on the cross to win salvation for us.

Opening Worship

Read in unison Psalm 119:161–68.

> Rulers persecute me without cause,
>   but my heart trembles at Your word.
> I rejoice in Your promise
>   like one who finds great spoil.
> I hate and abhor falsehood
>   but I love Your law.
> Seven times a day I praise You
>   for Your righteous laws.
> Great peace have they who love Your law,
>   and nothing can make them stumble.
> I wait for Your salvation, O LORD,
>   and I follow Your commands.
> I obey Your statutes,
>   for I love them greatly.
> I obey Your precepts and Your statutes,
>   for all my ways are known to You.

Introduction

Many people today have become "religious." They seek fulfillment in this life and a hope for a future after they die. They say,

"I am getting in touch with my spiritual self."

"I seek the guidance of a higher power."

"I am trying hard to live the perfect life."

Satan might delude these individuals into believing that their lives are more fulfilled and that they can look forward to a life after death just by being religious or spiritual, apart from Christ.

1. What ultimate consequence do these people face?

51

2. Why do you think that salvation by His grace through faith in Jesus is at times "foolishness" to those seeking fulfillment in this life and assurance of life after death?

3. How can we witness our faith to those who seek religious fulfillment?

In today's session, God uses a young girl to witness His power to a high-ranking official suffering from an incurable skin disease. The remedy and cure seem unreasonable and illogical. But God's ways are not our ways, and through simple means God provides healing to Namaan and foretells the spiritual healing He offers to us.

Inform

Read 2 Kings 5:1–19.

About the Text

The story of Naaman's healing is set in Aram, a powerful nation located on the northern border of Israel. David once conquered the Arameans, but during Solomon's reign the leader and people of Aram regained their independence. Now, in the time of the divided kingdom, the Arameans frequently raid Israel's property and livestock. They pose a serious threat to the people of God and the nation's stability.

Naaman is commander of the Aramean army—an influential man, next in authority to King Ben Hadad. Yet Naaman lives under a dark cloud—an incurable skin disease. (*Leprosy* translated from Hebrew designates several different skin diseases, not necessarily leprosy as we know it.) Though persons in Israel who suffered from skin diseases were obligated by the law to live apart from the larger community, no such restrictions are placed upon Arameans. Despite his condition and his perhaps unsightly appearance, Naaman rises to a high position and commands the respect of his fellow citizens and soldiers.

The young Israelite girl is the victim of a raiding party; she is most likely sold to Naaman as a domestic slave. This tragic injustice, however, is quickly redeemed by God. The girl becomes a chosen instrument to accomplish the divine purpose. Her courage in speaking to the commander's wife is striking: she testifies to the living God, to His prophet Elijah, and to the miracles worked in the name of Israel's God.

As though by divine arrangement, Naaman believes the girl's word. He immediately requests a formal delegation to Joram, king of Israel. The purpose of the audience is simple: "Cure Naaman of his disease." Joram, of course, is mortified by the message; he interprets the demand as a pretext for war or a border dispute. He dismisses or ignores the power of God revealed in His prophet Elisha.

Elisha's faith in God and his sense of God-given authority and mission allow the prophet to address Joram directly. He knows the reason for Naaman's visit and is ready and able, by God's grace, to heal the commander. Yet God's ways do not always correspond to human expectations! The command to wash "seven times in the Jordan" appears to Naaman as hollow advice; surely a genuine man of God would require an elaborate rite as a means of healing. But Elisha's prescription is to call forth faith. He doesn't need to dazzle or amuse his audience. Naaman will be healed by the power of God, and the only response is to believe in and confess the true Creator and Savior of the world.

Naaman's reluctance to obey Elisha is overcome by the gentle persuasion of his attendants. When Naaman is healed—precisely as Elisha said—he returns with all his servants and acknowledges God as the only God. He even begs to be known as a believer in spite of the idolatrous duties he fulfills. Elisha refuses a gift from the Aramean leader, since God's gift of healing is free and without limit. Naaman's new faith finds expression in his desire to sacrifice to Israel's God even when he returns to his native Aram.

Though a believer, Naaman understands the obligations he faces as the king's officer and confidant. In the future he will stand in the temple of the Aramean god Rimmon to offer sacrifice for the welfare of the nation and its ruler. Yet his act of "worship" is meaningless; from now on, Naaman will serve the true God, though his duties might require his presence or participation at pagan rituals. In a fervent explanation to Elisha, Naaman asks for understanding and patience in his predicament. Elisha's dismissal, "Go in peace," signals the forgiveness and hope that God gives through faith.

Discussing the Text

1. Who is Naaman? What dark cloud hangs over the life of Naaman?

2. How does God use the injustice of the enslaving of the young Israelite girl to accomplish His divine purpose?

3. Why does Elisha's command to wash seven times in the Jordan River seem like hollow advice to Naaman?

4. What is the purpose of Elisha's prescription for healing?

5. How does Naaman's newfound faith find expression?

Connect

Naaman's disease is an indirect result of human sinfulness, an inevitable part of a fallen, decaying world. He suffers, not for his own sins, but as a human being who shares in the guilt of the first man and woman. He is a proud man, whose position and prestige in society blind him to God's quiet strength and grace. Naaman demands signs and wonders, impressive displays of authority. God's ways, however, are beyond human thought. Any attempt to manipulate God, to exploit His kindness for selfish human gain, will fail: "Do not be deceived: God cannot be mocked" (Galatians 6:7).

All healing and wholeness are divine gifts. In mercy God extends His blessing to His chosen people, without any merit or effort on our part. The key is love: "God demonstrates His own love for us in this: While we were still sinners, Christ died for us" (Romans 5:8; see also Ephesians 2:4). In His ministry, Jesus heals people with many different kinds of diseases as a sign of God's love toward His creation. His death on the cross brings us full healing—forgiveness and eternal salvation. Like Naaman, we have been washed in the waters of Holy Baptism and made a new creation: "The old has gone, the new has come!" (2 Corinthians 5:17).

The story of Naaman's healing celebrates God's grace at work in ordinary means: water and promise. Today the Lord still bestows His life-changing grace through water and the Word. In Baptism, God's people, including children of all ages, are brought into a covenant relationship. The forgiveness purchased at the cross and confirmed in the resurrection is granted to all who believe the Savior's Word: "I am the way and the truth and the life" (John 14:6). With one voice, the apostles proclaim the truth of God's healing and redeeming love in Holy Baptism. We are marked, sealed, and renewed as we are united to Christ.

1. How does God demonstrate that His ways are beyond human thought and understanding?

2. Disease is a result of human sinfulness. Healing and wholeness are divine gifts. How has God in Christ granted us full healing?

3. Similar to Naaman, how have we been washed clean and made new creations?

4. God works through simple means to heal Naaman. How does God continue to work through simple means today to provide healing and strength to sinners?

Vision

To Do This Week

Family Connection

1. Review the events of the healing of Naaman.

2. Point out how God used a young girl to accomplish His purpose. Ask, "How does God use children today to accomplish His purpose?"

3. Remember Baptism experiences. Talk about the cleaning, the thorough washing, that God has provided to each of us through Holy Baptism. In Baptism God cleanses us from our sin and makes us His own dear children.

4. Send Baptism birthday cards to family members and friends to help them remember how God worked mightily through water and His Word at their Baptisms.

Personal Reflection

1. Consider how God has cleansed you from the deadly disease—sin.

2. Thank God for the washing and renewal of life He provided to you at your Baptism.

3. Think of at least one person with whom you can share the message of love and forgiveness won through Jesus' death on the cross. Pray that the Spirit will provide you the opportunity to witness your faith to that person. When the opportunity arises tell the person how God has worked in your life.

Closing Worship

Close with the following prayer adapted from the Order of Holy Baptism.

Almighty and most merciful God and Father, we thank and praise You that You graciously preserve and enlarge Your family and have granted us the new birth in Holy Baptism and made us members of Your Son, our Lord Jesus Christ, and an heir of Your heavenly kingdom. We humbly beseech You that, as we have become Your children, You will keep us in our baptismal grace so that according to all Your good pleasure, we may faithfully grow to lead a godly life to the praise and honor of Your name and, with all Your saints, obtain the promised inheritance in heaven; through Jesus Christ, our Lord. Amen.

For Next Week

Read 2 Kings 11:1–12:21 in preparation for the next session.

Joash Rules Judah

(2 Kings 11:1–12:21)

Focus

Theme: God in Control!

Law/Gospel Focus

At times sin may cause it to seem that God has lost His control of this world. But Jesus conquered sin, death, and the power of Satan through His death and resurrection. In Christ, God's people need not fear the present nor the future, but instead can rejoice in the forgiveness of sins and the eternal life that they have received by God's grace through faith.

Objectives

By the power of the Holy Spirit working through God's Word, we will
1. describe the events leading up to the reign of Joash and how God continues to demonstrate His divine control in life;
2. explain how the reign of Joash is ultimately used by God to fulfill His promise of the Messiah;
3. provide evidence of God's control in our lives;
4. describe how God has used events in our lives to fulfill His good and gracious purpose.

Opening Worship

Sing or speak together "Lord, Take My Hand and Lead Me."

Lord, take my hand and lead me
Upon life's way;

Direct, protect, and feed me
From day to day.
Without Your grace and favor
I go astray;
So take my hand, O Savior,
and lead the way.

Lord, when the tempest rages,
I need not fear;
For You, the Rock of Ages,
Are always near.
Close by Your side abiding,
I fear no foe,
For when Your hand is guiding,
In peace I go.

Lord, when the shadows lengthen
And night has come,
I know that You will strengthen
My steps toward home,
And nothing can impede me,
O blessed Friend!
So, take my hand and lead me
Unto the end.

Introduction

"Who's in charge here?"

1. In what circumstances might someone speak these words?

2. Describe events or situations that have occurred causing you to question whether God's in charge or in control in your life.

3. As you reflect back to the event, how did God ultimately reveal His control? How did God use the situation to further His kingdom?

In today's session we witness human beings who experience the tragic effects of the depravity of sin. But in all the situations that take place, God remains in control, ultimately using the events to further His will and His purpose. God is indeed in control!

Inform

Read 2 Kings 11:1–12:21.

About the Text

Joash, the young king of Israel, is born in 842 B.C., the son of Ahaziah. After the murder of his father, his paternal grandmother, Athaliah, seeks to destroy the whole royal family, including Joash. Yet God provides an escape for the young boy through his aunt: Jehosheba, Ahaziah's sister, hides Joash for six years in the priestly quarters of the temple.

Jehoiada, husband of Jehosheba and uncle of Joash (2 Chronicles 22:11), is a faithful priest in the service of the Lord. When Joash is seven years old—an appropriate age to begin his reign—Jehoiada makes preparations for the boy to be acclaimed king. Under a cloak of secrecy and tight security, Joash appears before a public assembly and is crowned ruler of God's people in Judah. He is immediately hailed as the legitimate heir to his father's throne.

The coronation of the new king is, from Athaliah's perspective, an act of treason. Yet her own murderous behavior is now exposed and rejected by the people. The punishment for her crimes is just: death! (The guards are careful not to execute Athaliah within the temple precincts, so as not to defile God's house.)

Jehoiada solemnly renews God's covenant with His people, a covenant that was flagrantly broken by the idolatry and disobedience of Athaliah. Joash and the nation also renew their covenant relationship and pledge to observe the Lord's commands and decrees. Together they restore the worship of the true God and destroy the temple, the idols, and the priests of Baal.

An important task before the nation and king is to repair the Lord's temple after years of neglect and willful destruction. Joash authorizes the priests to draw from temple funds—the regular offerings brought by worshipers—to begin the process of restoring the exterior and interior to their original condition.

Over the next 20 years, however, little or no progress is made on the temple repairs. As a result, Joash summons Jehoiada and the priests, who commission skilled craftsmen to carry on the project. This new focus in organization and responsibility allows valuable resources to go directly to workers, who act with integrity toward the Lord and His house of worship.

As king, Joash's success and faithfulness to God's covenant are linked with the influence of Jehoiada: "Joash did what was right in the eyes of the LORD all the years Jehoiada the priest instructed him" (12:2). After the priest's death, though, Joash becomes tolerant of Baal worship and even kills Zechariah, Jehoiada's son and his own cousin, a prophet sent by God to warn the king to turn from his wicked ways (2 Chronicles 24:17–22). Later, when Jerusalem is threatened by Hazael, king of Aram, Joash resorts to a shameless act to "buy" his and the city's freedom—he gives away as ransom all the sacred vessels and furnishings, as well as the substantial funds, from the temple, rather than trusting in God to provide protection.

Discussing the Text

1. How does God demonstrate His control even as Athaliah schemes to destroy the royal family?

2. Why is Joash crowned ruler of God's people under a cloak of secrecy and tight security?

3. How does Joash follow the lead of the priest Jehoiada in renewing the covenant between God and His people?

4. What occurs after the death of the priest Jehoiada?

Connect

God's Law forbids murder. The history of the kings of Israel and Judah reads, at times, like a tabloid report of violent acts and wrongful deaths. Athaliah's story is no different, but her crimes—the murder of her grandchildren!—are also flagrant violations of the social order (a felony offense in modern terms). Above all, her wickedness is an affront to the holy God, who alone has the right to give and take life. God speaks clearly and forcefully in His Word: "You shall not murder." Yet because of greed and hatred and selfish desire, human beings have killed one another from the beginning of creation. She was also overthrowing God's appointed rulers.

The priests also seem to have broken faith with God's Word and worship by their indifference toward the temple repairs. Whether a matter of apathy or inability, God's house languishes for more than 20 years in neglect and disrepair.

The plot to kill Joash is not merely a threat to the political stability of the kingdom. At stake is God's promise to send the Messiah, the son of David, to rule as king of Israel. Joash, David's descendant, is an essential link to the fulfillment of the Lord's ancient Word to His people. Athaliah's apparent victory, then, is both empty and brief, because God controls the course of history and works all things according to His purpose in Christ. In the fullness of time, St. Paul writes, "God sent His Son, born of a woman, born under law, to redeem those under law, that we might receive the full rights of sons" (Galatians 4:4–5). The Savior, Jesus Christ, is both Son of God and Son of David, fully divine and fully human. The Gospel proclaims the incarnation, ministry, suffering, death, and resurrection of Jesus, the fulfillment of the Law and the prophets. In Christ, God's people rejoice in the hope of forgiveness and eternal life.

God protects and strengthens Joash to carry out His plan to redeem the world through Christ. While still a child, Joash begins his reign under God's blessing and the godly example of guardians and relatives. The Lord's chosen path and grand purpose for our lives is not always evident, but we walk through danger and difficulty all the way. As St. Paul acknowledged, "We must go through many hardships to enter the kingdom of God" (Acts 14:22). Yet as our loving Father greets us at heaven's door, we see that the Savior has walked with us all along, guiding, protecting, and working His plan. In Christ, we are more than conquerors!

1. What occurs in the Scripture account when people no longer listen to or follow God's Word? What occurs today when people no longer listen to or follow God's Word?

2. What evidence do we have from the story that God controls the course of history and works all things according to His purpose

in Christ? What evidence do you have in your life that God works all things according to His purpose?

3. At times the Lord's chosen path and grand purpose for our lives is not always evident. Give examples from your life. How does the eternal life Jesus won for us on the cross give us hope and comfort as we face hardships and troubles in this life?

Vision

To Do This Week

Family Connection

1. Review how God protects and preserves Joash. Then discuss how God has protected and preserved you.

2. God demonstrates the importance of His Word in the story of Joash. Through God's Word, the Holy Spirit strengthens saving faith so that we can withstand the temptations we encounter. Ask, "Why is it important for us to read and study God's Word regularly?"

3. Consider ways in which your family can stay better connected to God's Word (e.g., family devotions, Bible reading, mealtime prayers).

Personal Reflection

1. Spend time meditating on God's activity in your life.

2. Consider new opportunities you may have to study God's Word.

3. Thank God for giving us His Word, through which the Holy Spirit works to strengthen faith.

Closing Worship

Speak together in unison the words of Psalm 119:105–112.

> Your Word is a lamp to my feet
> > and a light for my path.
> I have taken an oath and confirmed it,
> > that I will follow Your righteous laws.
> I have suffered much;
> > preserve my life, O LORD, according to Your Word.
> Accept, O LORD, the willing praise of my mouth,
> > and teach me Your laws.
> Though I constantly take my life in my hands,
> > I will not forget Your law.
> The wicked have set a snare for me,
> > but I have not strayed from Your precepts.
> Your statues are my heritage forever;
> > they are the joy of my heart.
> My heart is set on keeping Your decrees
> > to the very end.

For Next Week

Read Jonah 1:1–4:11 in preparation for the next session.

Session 8

Jonah Preaches God's Word in Nineveh

(Jonah 1:1–4:11)

Focus

Theme: No Limit to God's Grace

Law/Gospel Focus

Because of our sinful nature, we cannot fathom the magnitude of God's love and mercy for all people. Thinking that His love is limited or exclusive may cause us to share His love and forgiveness only with those we consider worthy. But God desires *all* people to be saved and sent His Son Jesus into the world to suffer and die for all people. God's love and forgiveness through faith in Christ Jesus equips and empowers us to share His love with all people, demonstrating that there is no limit to His grace.

Objectives

By the power of the Holy Spirit working through God's Word, we will
1. describe significant events in the account of Jonah;
2. explain the reason Jonah disobeys God's command;
3. summarize how God transforms and uses Jonah to accomplish His will and purpose;
4. praise God for His unlimited grace, shown to us in Christ Jesus;
5. seek new opportunities to share God's grace—which has no limit—with those who might be considered unworthy.

Opening Worship

Pray together the following prayer for steadfast faith:
Almighty God, our heavenly Father, through Your tender

love toward us sinners You have given us Your Son so that, believing in Him, we might have everlasting life. Continue to grant us Your Holy Spirit so that we may remain steadfast in this faith to the end and come to life everlasting; through Jesus Christ, our Lord. Amen.

Introduction

"We seek good members to join our church."

"As our neighborhood has changed, we have considered moving our congregation to a new location so that we can better serve our church family and attract new members."

"Our congregation has developed a strong family ministry. We have considered sponsoring events for divorced individuals, but don't want to give the message that we affirm divorce."

1. How might these statements limit God's grace?

2. What other statements or actions by Christians might limit God's grace?

3. Discuss the statement that there is "No limit to God's grace." What are the implications of affirming this statement? How can it affect your congregation?

"No limit to God's grace" is the main message of the account of Jonah. While Jonah attempts to limit God's grace to His people,

God has other plans through which He transforms the hearts and lives of sinners.

Inform

Read Jonah 1:1–4:11.

About the Text

Jonah is called to be the Lord's prophet during the reign of Jeroboam II, one of the most powerful kings in the history of ancient Israel (793–753 B.C.). He is a contemporary of Amos, Joel, and Hosea, prophets in the Northern Kingdom, and Isaiah and Micah, prophets in the Southern Kingdom. Yet Jonah has a rather distinctive mission: to speak God's Word to foreigners, namely the people of Nineveh.

Jonah, whose name means "Dove," lives in Gath Hephet, a small town near Nazareth in the northern part of Israel. Nineveh, in contrast, is situated on the Tigris River, 500 miles from Jerusalem. Nineveh was the capital of the Assyrian Empire, a thriving metropolis with magnificent buildings, high culture, a robust economy, and a population of more than 100,000 people. (Later, Nineveh is destroyed by a coalition of Medes and Babylonians in 612 B.C.) Thus, Jonah's mission calls him from an obscure village to the premier city of the ancient world.

Jonah's reason for disobeying God and running away from His call is disclosed only near the end of the story. In truth, Jonah seeks to limit God's grace to his own nation. Perhaps he reflects the strong sense of community identity among the Israelites and the conviction that God has redeemed Israel alone to be His chosen people. The confession of faith, "a gracious and compassionate God, slow to anger and abounding in love," should remain, in the prophet's view, a guarded secret within his own country.

Jonah's plan to travel from Joppa, a seaport town 35 miles northwest of Jerusalem, to Tarshish, a mining village in Spain, illustrates his utter avoidance of God's mission. Yet the Lord determines the course of history and the path every person takes; He controls the forces of nature and turns the outcome in spite of human rebellion and disobedience. The "violent storm" almost brings the voyage to an immediate close. When Jonah is identified as the cause of the tempest—the casting of lots is a common practice to discern God's will (Proverbs 16:33)—Jonah acknowledges his guilt before God and the crew.

Repentant, Jonah is willing to lose his life in order to save the ship (in that day, to capsize in the Mediterranean was almost always a major disaster, resulting in a total loss of life). The sailors are reluctant to cast a passenger overboard, but after exhausting their skill and strength they are left with no choice. Pleading for Jonah's God to not hold them accountable, they throw Jonah into the sea—a terrifying end! The storm stops as quickly as it started.

The "great fish" that swallows Jonah is God's means to preserve His servant for the mission to Nineveh. Through all of Jonah's efforts to escape his calling, God is still working to accomplish His purpose. Jonah's prayer attests to the prophet's acceptance of the Lord's righteous discipline ("You hurled me into the deep," 2:3), but also to his unwavering confidence in God's salvation ("You brought my life up from the pit, O LORD my God," 2:6). Jonah learns that God's grace and compassion extend, first of all, to his own desperate need. His words are marked by thanksgiving and praise, not fear and doubt, for God's promise will be fulfilled. Jonah is safe in God's care.

Jonah most likely returns to Joppa to begin his second journey to Nineveh. He had heard the call of God again, and He is strengthened for the task with the Lord's assurance, "Proclaim … the message I give you" (3:1). Jonah is a herald, an ambassador to the king and people of Nineveh, sent by the authority and with the message of the King of the universe.

As Jonah soon learns, God's Word is indeed powerful. His mission comes to a successful conclusion when the people of Nineveh, from the king to beggars, believe God, repent of their wickedness, fast, and call upon God to be merciful and forgive their sins. The Lord's promise does not fail, but bears abundant fruit by His blessing and purpose (Isaiah 55:10–11). God always shows compassion to His repentant people. In mercy He removes the guilt of the guilty and pardons those deserving of punishment. Jonah, the reluctant prophet, does not fear opposition to his mission as much as its genuine reception. His complaint focuses on the Lord's readiness to forgive and restore. In response, God illustrates for

Jonah the nature of compassion: as Jonah is concerned for a mere vine, so the creator of the universe cares for all people, young and old, the righteous and the wicked. Though Jonah—and all humankind—may be quick to reject and condemn, God, in limitless mercy, desires every person to know His love and salvation.

Discussing the Text

1. Why does Jonah disobey God and run away from his call?

2. How does Jonah avoid God's mission?

3. How does God demonstrate His control of the course of history and nature to work His will and purpose?

4. How does Jonah demonstrate repentance?

5. How does Jonah learn of the power of God's Word?

6. Why does Jonah complain to the Lord? How does God demonstrate to Jonah the true nature of compassion?

Connect

Jonah's mission and his life reflect God's fervent desire to call His people to repentance through His Word. The proclamation of the Law takes on personal significance for Jonah because he knows God's power, authority, and purpose stand behind the message of judgment. Through the Law, God confronts and humbles sinful humankind; through the Law, God exposes the rift between His majesty and righteousness and our selfish, wicked thoughts and actions. By the light of God's holy Law, our brightest achievement is complete darkness. God speaks His Law, St. Paul writes, "so that every mouth may be silenced, and the whole world may be held accountable" (Romans 3:19). No one earns, barters for, or buys salvation through the Law.

The Gospel of love and forgiveness is the heart of Jonah's story. Though afraid of his calling to share the Good News, Jonah is a true preacher of God's limitless grace. The prophets of the Old Testament all share the task of announcing the world's redeemer, promised to Israel and revealed in the person of Jesus of Nazareth. His suffering and crucifixion are the definitive display of God's passion to redeem His people from slavery to sin, death, and hell. The eternal Father willingly gives up His only Son unto death so that we might have forgiveness and life. God's salvation always finds fulfillment in Christ!

The Gospel is free, universal, and eternal. By Christ's own mandate, His people, the church, are to "make disciples of all nations" (Matthew 28:19). Baptism, instruction in the master's teaching, and the Lord's presence in Word and Sacrament are the means to reach out to and embrace the world with forgiveness and hope. No discrimination exists or should exist in the community of the redeemed, for God shows no favoritism (Acts 10:34; Romans 2:11). Nor does God direct His servants only to select ethnic and national groups. The God who desires all people to be saved calls and equips His church to preach repentance and forgiveness of sins in Christ to all nations, beginning in Jerusalem but extending to all parts of the earth (Luke 24:47). In all facets of daily life and work, His people are messengers of hope.

1. Why does God speak His Law to the people of Nineveh? To people today?

2. How is Jonah a preacher of God's limitless grace? How does God continue to offer His limitless grace to people today?

3. How does God use people today to reach out and embrace the world with forgiveness of sins and eternal life? How can we as members of Christ's church be messengers of hope to our community? To our nation? To the world?

Vision

To Do This Week

Family Connection

1. Have family members each draw a picture depicting a different portion of the account of Jonah.

2. How might we at times try to limit God's grace? What might we do to keep from limiting God's grace?

3. Pray that the Holy Spirit will empower you to witness boldly your faith in Jesus with family, friends, and all other people.

Personal Reflection

1. Consider, "Who is the most difficult person for you to love?" Pray that the Holy Spirit working through the Gospel will empower and motivate you to demonstrate love to that person.

2. "Limitless grace." Meditate on the significance of this in your life.

Closing Worship

Sing or speak together the following stanzas of "Love in Christ Is Strong and Living."

> Love in Christ is strong and living,
> Binding faithful hearts in one;
> Love in Christ is true and giving.
> May His will in us be done.
>
> Love is patient and forbearing,
> Clothed in Christ's humility,
> Gentle, selfless, kind, and caring,
> Reaching out in charity.
>
> Love in Christ abides forever,
> Fainting not when ills attend;
> Love, forgiving and forgiven,
> Shall endure until life's end.

For Next Week

Read Isaiah 6:1–8; 9:1–6; 2 Kings 4:8–17 in preparation for the next session.

Session 9

God Calls Isaiah

(Isaiah 6:1–8; 9:1–6; 2 Kings 4:8–17)

Focus

Theme: The Lord Saves

Law/Gospel Focus

Through His Law, God confronts us with His holiness and reveals the depth of human depravity and our deficiency to do that which God commands. No one has the strength or merit to stand before God. Only by God's grace—undeserved love—revealed in the person and work of Jesus Christ can we approach God in faith. Through Jesus' death on the cross, we have full access to God's love and forgiveness. God's love empowers and equips us to serve Him.

Objectives

By the power of the Holy Spirit working through God's Word, we will
1. describe the events of the call of Isaiah;
2. explain the reason for Isaiah's initial response to God's call;
3. compare Isaiah's call to our own call to faith;
4. confess boldly God's grace revealed in and through the person and work of Jesus.

Opening Worship

Sing or speak together "Isaiah, Mighty Seer, in Spirit Soared."

> Isaiah, mighty seer, in spirit soared
> And saw enthroned in majesty the Lord,
> Around whose throne shone glory from His face,
> Whose robe of light filled all the holy place.
> Beside the throne two six-winged seraphim,

Who with their wings showed reverence to Him.
With two each hid his face in holy awe,
With two his feet, these angels without flaw,
And with the third wing pair ascended high
To span the heavens with this mighty cry:
"Holy is God, the Lord of Sabaoth!
Holy is God, the Lord of Sabaoth!
Holy is God, the Lord of Sabaoth!
His grace and might and glory fill the earth!"
Then shook the roof beam and the lintel stone,
And smoke of incense swirled around the throne.

Introduction

1. Parents give their children names for various reasons. What are some reasons parents might give their child a certain name?

2. Share the reason for the name your parents gave you.

3. In today's session, we will study the call of Isaiah. Isaiah means "the Lord saves." What is the significance of Isaiah's name? What do you know about Isaiah and his message that explains the appropriateness of his name? At the end of today's session, return to this question to see if you can list additional reasons that Isaiah's name was appropriate.

Inform

Read Isaiah 6:1–8 and 9:1–6.

About the Text

Isaiah, whose name means "the Lord saves," is sometimes considered to be Israel's greatest prophet. His message presents a bold witness to God's righteous judgment, abundant grace, and promise of salvation in the Messiah. Born to a prominent family, Isaiah begins his prophetic career under King Uzziah (740 B.C.) and serves the Lord under the kings Jotham, Ahaz, and Hezekiah (almost 60 years). God first speaks to the prophet through a spectacular vision of His divine majesty and glory. This solemn revelation both calls and equips Isaiah for a life of service to the Lord Almighty.

Isaiah portrays the heavenly scene in vivid language and imagery. The seraphs are supernatural beings who worship before the throne of God. The chorus shakes the temple to its foundations; the cry, "Holy, holy, holy," testifies to the triune nature of the living God. Each person of the Trinity is worthy of glory and majesty and adoration.

Isaiah's response to the vision of God is utter humility and awe. In the presence of the holy and omnipotent God, sinful humankind may only cry out in despair. Isaiah knows and confesses without hesitation that he is lost and condemned; he stands completely at the mercy of the eternal God.

Yet God does not destroy His servant: He forgives. In love and undeserved favor, God reaches out—through the seraph's tong and hot coal—to remove the prophet's sin and guilt. Isaiah is both redeemed, purchased back from slavery to disobedience and the devil, and renewed, strengthened for the tasks of his ministry to God's people. When God announces His mission, Isaiah is ready and able to respond, "Here am I. Send me!"

Isaiah's assignment is to speak both God's Law and His Gospel. To a rebellious, stubborn people, he proclaims a word of judgment. Yet the prophet always includes God's word of grace for His chosen nation. The prophecy of the royal Son, who reigns on the throne of David, is a striking illustration of God's promise for a glorious future.

The land of Zebulun and Naphtali is northern Israel. Once the victims of Assyrian domination, the inhabitants will see a "great light" as God comes to rescue His people from the darkness of sin and death. Isaiah is convinced that God's Word is reliable; the promise will be fulfilled. The time of the Messiah, though still in the future, is also already a present certainty. Isaiah then addresses God in a direct hymn of praise, because His power to deliver His people from oppression in the past will be again revealed as He liberates the nation from spiritual bondage. The coming of the Messiah brings an end to slavery, wrath, punishment, and condemnation. His salvation is perfect and complete.

The birth of the messianic child is perhaps the most celebrated of God's promises in the Holy Scriptures. The Son of God, from eternity with the Father, becomes fully human for the salvation of the whole world. Isaiah portrays His origin and mission in grand titles and picturesque language. The child is the fulfillment of God's sacred pledge; He is a gift, a royal figure who rules His people with God's authority and power. His majestic names reveal His identity and purpose. As "Wonderful Counselor," He is divine Wisdom, sent forth to accomplish the royal plan for the redemption of God's dear children. As "Mighty God," He possesses all the attributes of the Trinity. As "Everlasting Father," He is the eternal, living God, whose fatherly care and faithfulness sustain His people through the arduous journey of life. As "Prince of Peace," He is the ruler who banishes hostility from His kingdom and restores the relationship between the King and His subjects.

Discussing the Text

1. What is the significance of the meaning of Isaiah's name—"the Lord saves"?

2. Describe the vision of God as seen by Isaiah.

3. Describe Isaiah's response to the vision of God.

4. How does God ready Isaiah for His mission so that Isaiah can reply, "Here am I. Send me!"?

5. How does Isaiah share the message of God's salvation and in so doing foretell the coming Messiah?

Connect

God's call to Isaiah is framed from start to finish by grace. The Lord gives His prophet a glimpse into heaven and later commissions him for a demanding, yet noble, ministry. Isaiah, however, recognizes his total inadequacy before God. From his new awareness of God's glory and righteousness, Isaiah asks only for mercy.

Through His Law, God confronts people with His holiness and reveals the depths of human deficiency. No person has sufficient strength or merit to stand before God. Only by grace, revealed in Christ, can sinful human beings approach God in faith and humility. Through Jesus' death and resurrection, believers have full access to God's love and forgiveness. Christ has taken away our sin, our guilt, and our fear of rejection and death. His infinite mercy, bestowed in Baptism and renewed through His body and blood, is the source of our daily strength. He is always present as we serve in His name.

1. How is God's call to Isaiah framed by grace? How is God's call to us framed by grace?

2. What does God continue to accomplish through His Law? What does God provide to repentant sinners?

3. How can we as God's witnesses continue to share His Law and His Gospel?

Vision

To Do This Week

Family Connection

1. The call of Isaiah gives us a glimpse into heaven. Have each family member draw a picture of heaven based upon Isaiah 6:1–8.

2. Discuss, "Why is it important for us to share the Good News of Jesus Christ with others?"

3. Seek new opportunities as a family to share your faith in Jesus with others.

4. Say, "God called you to be His servant." Ask, "When did God choose you as His servant?" Allow time for family members to respond. Then say, "At your Baptism God chose you to be His own dear child to receive the forgiveness of sins and eternal life. As His child you will naturally desire to share His love with others."

Personal Reflection

1. Pull out memorabilia from your Baptism. Read letters, cards, the church bulletin, and other items you may have saved. Thank God for choosing you to be His own dear child. Pray that you will boldly proclaim the Good News of Jesus Christ.

2. Consider the purpose of God's Law and the purpose of God's Gospel. Praise God for His Word, through which the Holy Spirit works to create and to strengthen saving faith.

Closing Worship

Pray together the following prayer:

Heavenly Father, God of all grace, waken our hearts that we may never forget Your blessings but steadfastly thank and praise You for all Your goodness so that we may live in Your fear until, with all Your saints, we praise You eternally in Your heavenly kingdom; through Jesus Christ, our Lord. Amen.

For Next Week

Read 2 Kings 18:1–20:11 in preparation for the next session.

Session 10

Hezekiah Prays to God

(2 Kings 18:1–20:11)

Focus

Theme: Comfort and Hope in Times of Crisis

Law/Gospel Focus

No one can save himself, deliver herself from the threat of eternal condemnation, or overcome the constant assaults of Satan and the world. God acts to save His people. In Christ, God has conquered the enemy and won the battle for all people. Jesus brings comfort and hope in times of crisis. Under Christ's protective care, we can endure temptation and trouble, confident that He will lead us home—to heaven.

Objectives

By the power of the Holy Spirit working through God's Word, we will
1. summarize how God's grace is evident in the life of Hezekiah;
2. describe how God enables Hezekiah to confess boldly his faith, even as he faces trials and temptations;
3. identify signs of God's grace in our own life;
4. face times of crisis with comfort and hope as we rely upon God's protective care and His promise to lead us home to heaven.

Opening Worship

Sing or speak together the following stanzas of "I Walk in Danger All the Way."

I walk in danger all the way.
The thought shall never leave me
That Satan, who has marked his prey,

Is plotting to deceive me.
This foe with hidden snares
May seize me unawares
If I should fail to watch and pray.
I walk in danger all the way.

I pass through trials all the way,
With sin and ills contending;
In patience I must bear each day
The cross of God's own sending.
When in adversity
I know not where to flee,
When storms of woe my soul dismay,
I pass through trials all the way.

I walk with Jesus all the way,
His guidance never fails me;
Within His wounds I find a stay
When Satan's pow'r assails me;
And by His footsteps led,
My path I safely tread.
No evil leads my soul astray;
I walk with Jesus all the way.

My walk is heav'nward all the way;
Await, my soul, the morrow,
When God's good healing shall allay
All suff'ring, sin, and sorrow.
Then, worldly pomp, begone!
To heav'n I now press on.
For all the world I would not stay;
My walk is heav'nward all the way.

Introduction

1. Reflect upon the stanzas of the hymn. What dangers have you or are you facing?

2. Recall how God has walked beside you in other times of trial, temptation, or hardship.

3. Read together Psalm 23. What assurance does God provide you as you face crises in your life?

Inform

Read 2 Kings 18:1–20:11.

About the Text

By God's grace, Hezekiah serves the people of Judah as a godly ruler and effective military leader. The son of King Ahaz, one of the most wicked kings, Hezekiah is influenced by his devout mother and God's prophets during his reign. His name, which means "Yahweh strengthens" in Hebrew, reveals the source of his conviction and spiritual integrity. Though a man of faith like his ancestor David, Hezekiah, also like David, is still a sinful man with human weaknesses. In particular, Hezekiah later in life is plagued by pride and ambition. Yet in His mercy, God blesses Hezekiah to the day of his death with faith and quiet hope in His Word.

Hezekiah's life and career are characterized in a brief, yet powerful statement: "Hezekiah trusted in the LORD, the God of Israel. There was no one like him among all the kings of Judah, either before him or after him" (2 Kings 18:5). Under his leadership, the doors of the Lord's temple are again opened; the priests remove the idols from the sanctuary and sanctify God's house for public worship. Hezekiah calls the nation to repentance and genuine faith and obedience in the living God. He also reinitiates the Passover celebration—practiced for the first time since Solomon ruled over the united kingdom. He destroys the shrines and images of popular religion and even breaks into pieces the bronze serpent. (Some in Israel have taken to worshiping the symbol.) God blesses His people through Hezekiah, and for a time Judah enjoys prosperity and success under its righteous king.

Although Hezekiah struggles with pride in later life, he does not fall into gross idolatry. Confident of God's help, he declares Judah an independent nation and wins freedom from old enemies. His national reforms are largely successful. But at times he relies upon his own insight and skill and neglects to ask God for wisdom and strength.

Hezekiah's first "test of faith" is an invasion of Judah by King Sennacherib of Assyria. In typical diplomatic fashion, Hezekiah immediately offers tribute to the powerful Assyrian army. The gesture gains time but little else. Sennacherib is soon standing at the gates of Jerusalem, demanding not simply money, but the city, its people, and king!

The speech by the Assyrian military delegation is designed to break down the morale of the troops and citizens of Jerusalem. The words are, of course, lies and propaganda. But the threats make a somber impression upon the people of God. The Assyrian army mocks the God of Israel, challenges the people's faith, and threatens the city with total destruction. The warning, "Do not listen to Hezekiah, for he is misleading you when he says, 'The LORD will deliver us' " (2 Kings 18:32), strikes at the heart of their trust in God's purpose. Yet the people maintain their confidence in the Lord and His chosen servant Hezekiah.

When word of the Assyrian taunt reaches King Hezekiah, he humbles himself in repentance and prayer. Perhaps Hezekiah views the crisis as the Lord's judgment upon the nation's sins. He quickly seeks the counsel of the Lord's prophet Isaiah. The response is encouraging: the Lord, not Sennacherib, will triumph. The living God will protect His chosen people.

Though the Assyrian messengers again mock Hezekiah's resolve, the king enters the temple to petition God to preserve his land and destroy the insolent foe. The Lord's answer comes through Isaiah: "I will defend this city and save it" (19:34). Previously God had allowed Sennacherib to conquer nations. But now God has drawn the line: the Assyrian army will be devastated and will return home in shame. God's Word is sure! His judgment upon the invasion force is swift, and Sennacherib's generals depart in disgrace, with only a remnant of their past resources.

Years later, Hezekiah stands on the verge of death. Isaiah's verdict, "You will not recover," is bitter truth. Hezekiah calls upon God to remember His covenant faithfulness and to look upon his past devotion to the Lord's Word and ways. God summons Isaiah to report to the king His mercy and protection for another 15 years. (God also promises deliverance from a future Assyrian invasion.)

While Isaiah declares and even demonstrates God's healing, Hezekiah asks for additional proof. The "sign" is a unique event in history: the shadow returns 10 steps, that is, moves suddenly backwards on the stairway of Ahaz. God, as the creator of light, time, and matter, suspends the ordinary laws of nature to accomplish His purposes.

The motive for Hezekiah's willingness to open the royal treasury for inspection is unknown. Isaiah views the action as foolish and disobedient to God (perhaps an indication of Hezekiah's pride). In time, the Babylonians do invade Judah to destroy the temple, plunder the treasury, and carry off the majority of the people to exile. The prophet's judgment, "Nothing will be left," is literally fulfilled.

Discussing the Text

1. What does Hezekiah's name mean? How does Hezekiah's name reveal the source of his conviction and spiritual integrity?

2. What is accomplished under Hezekiah's leadership?

3. With what sin does Hezekiah struggle?

4. How is Hezekiah's faith tested?

5. What unique sign does God provide as proof of Hezekiah's healing?

Connect

God alone is the Savior of His chosen servants. Hezekiah's rule and accomplishments are a perfect illustration of "God's abundant provision of grace" (Romans 5:17). In his lifetime, Hezekiah is often threatened with annihilation. A hostile, superior enemy, a mysterious fatal illness, and many other dangerous situations bring to light his complete helplessness. He cannot, even with the best human resources, save himself or his nation. The reality of sin and suffering, danger and destruction are all too apparent. Hezekiah stands in dire need of God's mercy.

The Law discloses the universal human condition: no one can save himself. No one can deliver herself from the threat of eternal condemnation. No one can overcome the constant—and always fatal—assaults of Satan and the world, assaults that result in sin and danger and death. The Gospel, however, proclaims that God has acted to save His people. In Christ, God has conquered the enemy and won the battle for the eternal destiny of humanity. St. Paul rejoices, "He forgave us all our sins. … And having disarmed the powers and authorities, He made a public spectacle of them, triumphing over them by the cross" (Colossians 2:13, 15). The victory that Hezekiah experiences by God's grace is now the final victory for all God's people: the victory of salvation in Jesus.

The Gospel brings comfort and hope in our own times of crisis. Under Christ's protective care, we endure temptation and trouble because our Lord and Savior walks with us. He is present in His Word and Sacrament. His promise sustains us, even when we feel overwhelmed by the opposition. His grace, through every trial and threat, will lead us home.

1. How does God demonstrate in the life of Hezekiah that He alone is the Savior of His chosen servants? How does God demonstrate in your life that He alone is your Savior?

2. Compare and contrast the purpose of the Law and the Gospel.

3. What is the victory that Hezekiah ultimately experiences? How is it the same victory for all who possess faith in Christ Jesus?

4. How does the Gospel bring comfort and hope in your times of crisis?

Vision

To Do This Week

Family Connection

1. Review the events in the account of Hezekiah.

2. Ask, "How is God's power evident in the life of Hezekiah?"

3. Like us, Hezekiah is a sinner. What hope and comfort has God provided to us sinners through the death and resurrection of His only Son Jesus? How do you feel knowing that God accepts sinners?

4. Discuss how the eternal life Jesus won for us on the cross can provide us hope as we face crises.

Personal Reflection

1. Consider the consequence of your sin upon Jesus. Praise God for giving His only Son to death on the cross as payment for your sin.

2. Consider how God's Law and Gospel—revealed in Scripture—shape your life.

3. Look for opportunities to give the reason for the hope you have when difficult situations, hardships, or troubles arise in your life.

Closing Worship

Sing or speak the following stanzas of "Jesus Sinners Will Receive."

> Jesus sinners will receive;
> May they all this saying ponder
> Who in sin's delusions live
> And from God and heaven wander!
> Here is hope for all who grieve:
> Jesus sinners will receive.
>
> Jesus sinners will receive.
> Even me He has forgiven;
> And when I this earth must leave,
> I shall find an open heaven.
> Dying, still to Him I cleave—
> Jesus sinners will receive.

For Next Week

Read at least some portions of Jeremiah 1:1–19; 7:1–29; 18:1–12; 19:1–15; 20:1–6; 23:5–6; 28:1–17; 31:31–34; 37:1–39:18; 2 Chronicles 20:1–30 in preparation for the next session.

Session 11

God Works through Jeremiah and Jehoshaphat

(Jeremiah 1:1–19; 7:1–29; 18:1–12; 19:1–15;
20:1–6; 23:5–6; 28:1–17; 31:31–34; 37:1–39:18;
2 Chronicles 20:1–30)

Focus

Theme: Ready to Forgive

Law/Gospel Focus

All people by nature have turned away from God's commands. But God reveals His love for us in and through the person and work of Jesus, whereby He offers forgiveness of sins and eternal life to all. God is not only ready but eager to forgive all repentant sinners. His love for us in Christ Jesus empowers us to share His Law and His Gospel to those living in sin so that they too may experience His forgiving love.

Objectives

By the power of the Holy Spirit working through God's Word, we will
1. summarize God's message to the people spoken through His prophet Jeremiah;
2. describe events in the reign of Jehoshaphat and the reason for his success;
3. confess our sinful nature and sinful thoughts, words, and deeds;
4. proclaim the forgiveness Jesus won for us on the cross.

Opening Worship

Sing or speak the first stanza of "The Law of God Is Good and Wise" and the first stanza of "The Gospel Shows the Father's Grace."

The Law of God is good and wise
And sets His will before our eyes,
Shows us the way of righteousness,
And dooms to death when we transgress.

The Gospel shows the Father's grace,
Who sent His Son to save our race,
Proclaims how Jesus lived and died
that man might thus be justified.

Introduction

"I'm ready to ..."

1. Finish this statement with as many endings as possible.

2. Share a time when you were ready but others weren't. Describe the feeling you had when you were ready to ... , but others were not.

3. God is always ready to forgive. In today's session, Jeremiah shares God's readiness to forgive, but we see how the people

refuse to repent—they aren't ready. How do you suppose God responds to His people's rejection?

As you study today's session remember this question. Return to the question at the end of today's session and answer it again.

Inform

Skim Jeremiah 1:1–19; 7:1–29; 18:1–12; 19:1–15; 20:1–6; 23:5–6; 28:1–17; 31:31–34; 37:1–39:18; and 2 Chronicles 20:1–30.

About the Text

Jeremiah is one of four major prophets in the Old Testament (Isaiah, Jeremiah, Ezekiel, and Daniel). Born in the city of Anathoth, near Jerusalem, he is raised in a priestly family, most likely a descendant of the famous priest Abiathar (1 Kings 2:26). God calls Jeremiah to be a prophet in the reign of King Josiah (626 B.C.), and he serves the Lord faithfully for 40 years.

Jeremiah perhaps owns an estate outside Jerusalem, but during his ministry he lives in the city and speaks his message in or near the temple. He prophesies under five kings, of whom only Josiah (640–609 B.C.) is described as God-fearing. The rest—Jehoahaz, Jehoiakim, Jehoiachin, and Zedekiah—reject all the prophet's warnings. Jeremiah also faces opposition from false prophets and is a frequent target of ridicule and persecution for his faithfulness to God's Word. In the turbulent years prior to the Exile, Jeremiah's mission is routinely dangerous; he often comes close to losing his life. In all these circumstances, however, Jeremiah remains strong, by God's grace, to his calling and faith.

God chooses Jeremiah. The Lord provides the strength and skill for his ministry. In spite of his youth, Jeremiah is given the authority and the power to preach the Word as God's chosen ambassador.

God gives Jeremiah two signs to confirm his call: the branch of an almond tree and a large boiling kettle. Both images reveal the nature of his ministry to God's people. The Lord stands with the prophet at all times, but his message must include the truth of God's judgment—an invasion from the north (the Babylonians) as punishment for the nation's idolatry and disobedience.

Jeremiah is a preacher of repentance. The Lord is ready to forgive, not wanting to punish but to welcome the nation back into the covenant relationship and renew His people in their worship and service. The false prophets express the foolish dreams of their own hearts and minds. Jeremiah's word is God's Word. The consequences of rejecting God's Word are all too evident in the Northern Kingdom. The Lord punishes the 10 tribes for their brazen idol worship by allowing the Assyrians to destroy the tabernacle at Shiloh and the regions around Samaria. For this reason alone, Jeremiah's message is deadly serious. Yet the people continue to ignore God's truth and to tragically follow the false prophets.

The nation's rebellion is so notorious, God declares, that Jeremiah is forbidden to pray for his fellow citizens of Judah. The deliberate violations of God's commands and covenant decrees have sealed the nation's fate: "The Sovereign LORD says, 'My anger and My wrath will be poured out on this place' " (7:20). In particular, the people abuse God's gift of worship; they offer sacrifices to foreign gods and goddesses; and they abandon truth for falsehoods and deception. Despite his diligent efforts, Jeremiah meets with little success in calling the people to repentance. The judgment he threatens in his preaching will soon come true.

For a time, though, Jeremiah continues to proclaim God's Word. The prophet is held in contempt, rejected, and imprisoned. Yet by repudiating Jeremiah, the religious leaders and the people are, in truth, repudiating God. By refusing to heed the Lord's summons to return in faith and obedience, the nation is responsible for its own punishment.

Yet God does not totally abandon His people. He promises to make a new covenant (31:31–34), rooted not in the strength of the people's commitment but upon His love and mercy.

The younger children also learn about King Jehoshaphat of Israel, who lived years before Jeremiah. The account of Jehoshaphat's reign in 2 Chronicles 20 is longer than the account in 1 Kings (22:41–50). By inspiration of the Spirit, the chronicler sees in Jehoshaphat's attitudes and actions a reverence and trust in God and a willingness to serve God's people faithfully and justly. The Lord is with Jehoshaphat (2 Chronicles 17:3), the Lord "establishe[s] the kingdom under his control" (v. 5), and Jehoshaphat's "heart [is] devoted to the ways of the LORD" (v. 6). The king not only abolishes idolatry but introduces a national reform, dispatching officials, Levites, and priests throughout Judah to teach the people "the Book of the Law," that is, God's Word (vv. 7–9).

Yet Jehoshaphat is not perfect. He makes serious misjudgments in administering the kingdom. The marriage of his son Jehoram to Athaliah, daughter of Ahab (21:6), may be designed to unite the divided kingdom, but nothing good comes from the alliance. The chronicler records the near disaster from the joint military campaign against Syria (18:1–19:4).

Encouraged by the Syrian victory over Israel and Judah, several tribes west and south of the Dead Sea join forces in an attack on Jehoshaphat and the nation. The invading forces consist mainly of Moabites and Ammonites. As they round the southern end of the Dead Sea, they are reinforced by "some of the Meunites" (20:1).

The invaders push northward to En-Gedi (v. 2), only 15 miles from Jerusalem. When scouts report the location of the enemy army, Jehoshaphat "proclaim[s] a fast for all Judah" (v. 3). Before the public assembly at the temple (representative of the cities of Judah), the king leads his people in fervent prayer for God's mercy and help. He acknowledges the almighty power of God and God's deliverance of His people in the past. He recalls God's protection and the people's resolve to "stand in Your presence before this temple" and "cry out to You in our distress" (v. 9). The king pleads with God to see—and, by implication, to respond to—the danger the people face in this advancing army. Finally, Jehoshaphat humbly admits the nation's utter helplessness and total dependence on God. Together with the families of Judah, he prays, "We do not know what to do, but our eyes are upon You" (v. 12).

The "Spirit of the LORD," speaking through a prophet, announces the answer to the prayer: the outcome will be the victory of God. "The battle is not yours, but God's" (v. 15). As if the promised deliverance is already a reality, the king and the people worship the Lord, the Levites singing hymns of praise "with very loud voice" (v. 19).

Their faith in God's promise is not in vain. In the battle that follows, the army does not have to strike a single blow. The Lord confuses the enemy soldiers so that they destroy one another (v. 23). Jehoshaphat and his people do not forget to thank God. Taking the plunder to Jerusalem and their homes, they go immediately to the temple to praise the Savior God.

God promises to be with His people as a fortress and refuge against the forces of wickedness. His goodness and mercy are always available in Christ, who has delivered us from the kingdom of darkness and brought us into His kingdom, where He reigns with His forgiveness. Through Jesus, we know that we will be eternally safe through all the many crises we face in life.

Discussing the Text

1. Why does Jeremiah face opposition and danger in fulfilling God's mission? What are some dangers Jeremiah faces? What enables Jeremiah to remain strong in all these circumstances?

2. What two signs does God give to Jeremiah to confirm his call?

3. How do the people of Israel respond to Jeremiah's message? What are the consequences of their response?

4. What evidence do we have that God does not totally abandon His people? See Jeremiah 31:31–34.

5. What evidence in Jehoshaphat's life demonstrates a trust in God?

6. How does God provide Jehoshaphat a military victory without the army ever having to strike a blow? How does Jehoshaphat respond to the victory?

Connect

For Jeremiah, a prophet's preaching had only one goal: to call God's people to repentance and forgiveness. To speak God's Law—His word of judgment—always entails risk: rejection, conflict, even martyrdom. The reason is clear: all people, by nature, have turned away from God's commands. Without exception, humankind has chosen to follow the way of selfish pride and personal autonomy. (God even makes this offer to the prophet: "If you can find but one person who deals honestly and seeks the truth, I will forgive this city" [Jeremiah 5:1]. Absolutely no one, however, measures up to God's standard.) Jeremiah's task, then, is to confront the people with God's Word, bringing to them a knowledge of their sinfulness. Afterward God's Spirit works to renew and strengthen their faith.

Although many of the people of Judah refuse to repent, a small number—the remnant (23:3)—hear the message, implore God's forgiveness, and believe His promise to redeem His chosen people. For these individuals, Jeremiah is not simply a preacher of judgment and repentance; he is a messenger of God's Good News of salvation. At the heart of his Gospel proclamation is the coming Messiah, who institutes the new covenant in His death and resurrection. His mission, to redeem God's people from sin, death, and condemnation and to gather the flock together in one fellowship, is the central theme of Jeremiah's ministry. In the future, God will truly be present among His people, and through Christ, the only Son of the Father, He will reveal His love and compassion for the world.

Jeremiah's witness to Jesus is strong and sure. As Christians, we see God's plan unfolding in the redemption of the nation and the fulfillment of the ancient promise to bless all nations in Christ. By faith and through Baptism, we share in the blessing of eternal life. Our hope is in Christ, our Shepherd and Savior.

1. What goal does Jeremiah have in His preaching? How is this goal evident in your pastor's preaching? Why is that goal so important? Jeremiah is a messenger of God's Good News of salvation. How does your pastor demonstrate that he also is a messenger of Good News?

2. How do people today often respond to God in a manner similar to the people of Judah?

3. How do we see God's plan of salvation unfold in the Old Testament? How has God's plan of salvation been fulfilled? What do we share because of the fulfillment of God's plan of salvation in the person and work of Jesus Christ?

Vision

To Do This Week

Family Connection

1. Review the message of Jeremiah. Ask, "How does the message bring bad news? What good news does Jeremiah also share with the people?"

2. Read aloud some family devotions. Look for both the Law—God's expectations for us and our inability to do what God requires—and the Gospel—the Good News of what God has done for us in the person and work of Jesus.

Personal Reflection

1. Consider the importance of God's Law and Gospel in your life.

2. Pray that the Holy Spirit will enable you to share God's message of love and forgiveness with a friend or loved one.

3. Think about how unpopular the Law is at times. What makes the Law so unpopular? Note that without the Law, people would never know of their need for a Savior.

Closing Worship

Pray together the prayer for steadfast faith,

Almighty God, our heavenly Father, by Your tender love toward us sinners You have given us Your Son so that, believing in Him, we might have everlasting life. Continue to grant us Your Holy Spirit so that we may remain steadfast in this faith to the end and come to life everlasting; through Jesus Christ, our Lord. Amen.

For Next Week

Read Daniel 3:1–30 in preparation for the next session.

Session 12

God Saves Daniel's Three Friends

(Daniel 3:1–30)

--- **Focus** ---

Theme: Who Is Your God?

Law/Gospel Focus

All people by nature and choice bow down before the gods of personal success and fulfillment—materialism, sex, ambition, power, alcohol, drugs—the list is endless. God, however, does not abandon His people to their own selfish desires and deserved condemnation. In love He reaches down to reclaim His lost children from sin through the sacrifice of Jesus on the cross. By His grace, God empowers us to stand firm in our convictions and reflect His goodness in our thoughts, words, and deeds.

Objectives

By the power of the Holy Spirit working through God's Word, we will

1. summarize the events leading up to and including the arrest of Shadrach, Meshach, and Abednego;
2. describe how the Lord works through Nebuchadnezzar's ruthless decree to save His people and extend His promise of salvation to future generations;
3. confess the forgiveness Jesus won for us on the cross;
4. reflect His love in what we say and do.

Opening Worship

Speak in unison the Apostles' Creed.

> I believe in God, the Father Almighty, maker of heaven and earth.
> And in Jesus Christ, His only Son, our Lord,

who was conceived by the Holy Spirit,
born of the virgin Mary,
suffered under Pontius Pilate,
was crucified, died and was buried.
He descended into hell.
The third day He rose again from the dead.
He ascended into heaven and sits at the right
   hand of God
      the Father Almighty.
From thence He will come to judge the living and
   the dead.
I believe in the Holy Spirit,
the holy Christian Church,
the communion of saints,
the forgiveness of sins,
the resurrection of the body,
and the life everlasting. Amen.

Introduction

In the Apostles' Creed, we confess our faith in the one true God. At times we must admit that although our lips speak these words, our thoughts, words, and actions confess another god or gods.

1. What other gods do Christians often confess with their thoughts, words, and deeds?

2. The First Commandment says, "You shall have no other gods." God deserves to be number one in our lives. Anything or anyone that becomes number one in our lives other than God has become our god. How do these or can these other gods crowd out the one true God?

3. Read Romans 5:6–11. How does God who knows our weakness act in love on our behalf?

In today's session, three of God's prophets are challenged by the question "Who is your God?" In a bold demonstration of their faith, they are able to witness to the one true God in spite of the threat of death.

Inform

Read Daniel 3:1–30.

About the Text

The book of Daniel is a remarkable testimony to God's faithful love and protection for His chosen people. Each story takes place in the sixth century B.C. in Babylon. The great king and conqueror Nebuchadnezzar, who destroyed Jerusalem and deported the inhabitants of Judah to Babylon, learns the truth of the Sovereign of the universe, who guides all history toward His purpose and glory.

The precise date and location of Nebuchadnezzar's ceremony of the golden image are unknown. The list of royal officials, administrative staff, and other guests suggests a large gathering at a prominent city of the empire. The monument is 90 feet high by 9 feet wide and is likely a combination of wood, stone, and metal with a gold overlay. It also probably stands on a huge base in a conspicuous part of the community.

The ceremony is essentially an act of homage or worship to the king. In the ancient world, the gods of the victorious empires are viewed as more powerful than the gods of conquered people. Since Nebuchadnezzar is the most powerful king in the Near East, his gods are, by definition, the most powerful on earth. A refusal to bow down—to lie prostrate on the ground—is an act of treason, punishable by death.

The three Jewish youths, who have been transported from Judah to Babylon, are serving in high government positions. But because they are foreigners, Shadrach, Meshach, and Abednego have enemies within the court. These native officials, who likely serve as astrologers, bring public charges against the young men. Nebuchadnezzar is furious with the youths' refusal to worship the image but offers a second chance: bow down or burn!

The three men, however, stand firm in their faith and resolve to obey God. Under no circumstances will they pay homage to idols. Shadrach, Meshach, and Abednego understand the consequence of their decision, yet prefer death in the blazing furnace to denying the living God.

In a swift sentence, Nebuchadnezzar orders a ruthless punishment for the youths (the "seven times hotter than usual" decree demonstrates the king's anger and his desire to make an example of rebellious subjects). But God controls the fate of His servants. The "son of the gods" in the furnace is the Lord's messenger, an angel sent to defend and preserve Shadrach, Meshach, and Abednego from certain destruction. Nebuchadnezzar's response to God's mighty act of deliverance is itself only an affirmation of God's power; the king remains a polytheist—a worshiper of many gods— throughout his life. Yet the Lord does work through the king's decree to save His people and extend His gracious promise to future generations.

Discussing the Text

1. How does the book of Daniel testify to God's faithful love and protection for His chosen people?

2. Why does Nebuchadnezzar become furious with the three Jewish youths?

3. How do Shadrach, Meshach, and Abednego demonstrate their faith and obedience to God?

4. What ruthless punishment does Nebuchadnezzar order for the young men?

5. How does God deliver Shadrach, Meshach, and Abednego from destruction? How does Nebuchadnezzar respond to God's act of deliverance?

Connect

Like other prophets, the three young men have a specific mission to carry out, as God works to extend His saving Word and purpose throughout the world. Their influential positions in the Babylonian empire afford a platform to witness to their faith in the living God. When required to compromise their beliefs, Shadrach, Meshach, and Abednego, with God's mercy and strength, draw the line. The Law is clear: idolatry is sin. God speaks forcefully through His Word and leaves no room for negotiation: "You shall have no other gods before Me" (Exodus 20:3). All people, by nature and by choice, bow down before the gods of personal success and fulfillment. A myriad of idols, including materialism, sex, ambition, and power—the list is endless—battle for the human heart. Without exception, apart from God's grace, the idols win.

God, however, never abandons His people to their own selfish desires and deserved condemnation. In love, He reaches down to reclaim His lost children from sin and Satan's sway. The Gospel announces God's full, free pardon in the sacrifice of Jesus Christ on the cross. Our reckless pursuit of idols is forgiven. God declares us "not guilty" because the Savior of the world has taken upon Himself our punishment. Jesus is God's Son, who walks into the fiery furnace and saves us from eternal judgment. By faith, we understand that God calls and provides the strength for our daily service. By His grace, we are enabled to stand firm in our convictions and reflect His goodness in our witness.

1. What is the mission of the three young men? How is their mission identical to the mission God has given to you?

2. How can obedience to God's Law cause you to face persecution and/or rejection? Give evidence of this.

3. Give evidence that people continue to bow down before the gods of personal success and fulfillment.

4. God never abandons His people. What does He grant to us through our faith in Christ Jesus, in spite of our reckless pursuit of idols?

Vision

To Do This Week

Family Connection

1. Review the events of this popular Bible story.
2. Ask, "How does God protect us today?"
3. Ask, "What dangers might we face as we continue to remain steadfast in God's Word? How might obedience to God's Word be unpopular today?"
4. Have members of your family take turns retelling or acting out the events of the account from Daniel 3. Emphasize the fact that God is always in control.

Personal Reflection

1. Confess your reckless pursuit of gods of personal success and fulfillment.
2. Rejoice in the forgiveness Jesus won for you on the cross.
3. Ask God to help you rely upon the power of the Holy Spirit to enable you to remain faithful to God's Word, even when doing so causes you to become unpopular or to even face persecution. Remember, as you remain faithful, God uses that opportunity to witness boldly the power of God's love in Christ in your life.

Closing Worship

Sing or speak together the following stanza from "I Walk in Danger All the Way."

> I walk with Jesus all the way,
> His guidance never fails me;
> Within His wounds I find a stay
> When Satan's pow'r assails me;
> And by His footsteps led,
> My path I safely tread.
> No evil leads my soul astray;
> I walk with Jesus all the way.

For Next Week

Read 2 Chronicles 36:5–23; Psalm 137:1–4; and Daniel 6:1–28 and 9:1–19 in preparation for the next session.

Session 13

God Keeps His People Safe

(2 Chronicles 36:5–23; Psalm 137:1–4;
Daniel 6:1–28; 9:1–19)

Focus

Theme: The Price of Faith

Law/Gospel Focus

God condemns our mistaken devotion to created things rather than the Creator. Despite our sin, God is our gracious Savior through His crucified Son Jesus. Through Jesus' death on the cross, we are washed clean—given a new start by faith—and raised from the death of sin to live a new life in devotion to God.

Objectives

By the power of the Holy Spirit working through God's Word, we will
1. describe the details of the account of Daniel, who through God's power remains faithful even as he faces death;
2. summarize how God rescues Daniel from certain death;
3. confess our weak or nonexistent witness of faith in Jesus when we face persecution or ridicule;
4. praise God for rescuing us from the clutches of sin and death and enabling us to confess Jesus as Lord and Savior even as we face rejection, persecution, or ridicule.

Opening Worship

Speak in unison the words of Philippians 2:5–11.

Your attitude should be the same as that of Christ Jesus:
> Who, being in very nature God,
> > did not consider equality with God
> > something to be grasped,

but made Himself nothing,
    taking the very nature of a servant,
    being made in human likeness.
And being found in appearance as a man,
    He humbled Himself
    and became obedient to death—even death on a
        cross!
Therefore God exalted Him to the highest place
    and gave Him the name that is above every name,
that at the name of Jesus every knee should bow,
    in heaven and on earth and under the earth,
and every tongue confess that Jesus Christ is Lord,
    to the glory of God the Father.

Introduction

1. When have you found it easy to share your faith in Jesus? Why?

2. When have you found it difficult or impossible to share your faith in Jesus? Why?

3. What "cost" might you have to pay if you share your faith in Jesus?

In today's session we learn of Daniel, who because of his witness of faith faced a heavy "price"—a death sentence in the lions' den. Strengthened by God's love, Daniel faces death rather than reject the Creator for the created. God rescues Daniel from death. God through Christ has also rescued us from death, and through His love He empowers us to worship the Creator—His will and His ways—even as we face rejection, persecution, or ridicule.

Inform

Read 2 Chronicles 36:5–23; Psalm 137:1–4; and Daniel 6:1–28; 9:1–19.

About the Text

The final days of the kingdom of Judah are marked by invasion, idolatry, destruction, and deep sorrow. God's punishment against the nation is evident in the sequence of assaults on Jerusalem and the temple by Nebuchadnezzar, king of Babylon. The last kings, as noted in 2 Chronicles 36, all abandon the covenant with God. Indeed, the leaders, the priests, and the people as a whole are characterized as "unfaithful," rebelling against God's Word and defiling His sanctuary with pagan practices. As a result, the Lord permits the Babylonian army to conquer Jerusalem, destroy the temple, and kill or deport thousands of men, women, and children into captivity (586 B.C.). God's people are, from all appearances, defeated!

Yet 70 years after the first invasion, God raises up Cyrus, king of Persia, to rescue His people and return the nation to its homeland in Israel. While in Babylon, a remnant of God's chosen people remain faithful to His Word and pray daily for their day of restoration and renewal. God answers their prayer and opens the door for a return to Judah and a new beginning in faith.

The name Darius is perhaps a title for Cyrus or another name for Gubaru, a governor appointed by Cyrus over Babylon. The organization of the Persian empire is based upon distinct regions ruled by satraps. Daniel is an administrator, with two other individuals, over the satraps.

Darius's plan to make Daniel the senior administrator provokes jealousy among the other officials. Daniel's record is impeccable;

he is known for his efficiency and complete honesty. The only way, then, to discredit his service to the king is to attack his ultimate loyalties. Daniel's faith in God will not allow him to worship an idol or mere human being.

The king's decree provides the pretext to accuse Daniel of treason. Because the law is unalterable, Daniel is sentenced to die—on the same day as his trial before Darius. Yet Darius is grieved by the proceedings and the verdict against his loyal servant. His blessing, spoken as a prayer, asks God's blessing upon Daniel in the face of certain death.

God vindicates Daniel by rescuing His prophet from the den of lions. Darius, too, releases Daniel from the sentence of death and takes revenge upon the instigators of the whole affair. Like Nebuchadnezzar, King Darius is a polytheist who views his kingdom as the most powerful nation in the Near East. His letter to the nations simply acknowledges that God is worthy of praise and respect. Yet God is not simply "one lord among many" but the only true, living God. Daniel's remarkable deliverance is a sure sign that God alone rules and protects His people in the world.

Discussing the Text

1. How do the other officials discredit Daniel's service to the king?

2. How does the king's decree set the stage for the other officials to accuse Daniel of treason? How does Darius demonstrate grief at the sentence of Daniel to die?

3. How does God rescue Daniel from death?

4. How does King Darius respond to the rescue that God provides for Daniel?

Connect

Like his three friends, Daniel withstands the pressure to conform to pagan society and to worship idols—at the price of his personal comfort and security. He denounces the false gods of the nations and calls upon all people, including his fellow Jews, to turn in repentance and faith to the living God. The Lord of the universe is not able to be reflected in the work of human hands, and wood or stone or metal can never represent or display His glory. Moreover, God threatens in His Word to punish sinful humankind for worshiping the creation instead of the Creator. The Law condemns our mistaken devotion.

The Gospel is the assurance that, despite our sin, God is our gracious Savior through Jesus Christ. In our Lord's death and resurrection, we are washed clean—given a new start by faith—and raised from the death of sin to live a new life. Jesus calls us to follow in His footsteps as disciples, with our priorities rooted in His kingdom. He has promised to be present in His Word and His Sacraments, to strengthen us for a bold witness to His love and peace. Through Christ, we stand firm against the lures of a hostile world. Like Daniel, we trust His mighty power to save.

1. How do we at times worship the created rather than the Creator?

2. What assurance does God provide us through the Gospel, despite our sinful devotion?

3. How does Jesus remain present with us even today? How is this a comfort and strength to us as we face temptations from a hostile world?

Vision

To Do This Week

Family Connection

1. Review the account of Daniel in the lions' den.
2. Have family members draw pictures of the account and then describe in their own words what their pictures depict.
3. Find a new way to thank God for the protection and guidance He provides us at all times.

Personal Meditation

1. Consider events that have occurred in your life that you might call a "lions' den." How did God protect you as you faced these situations?
2. Praise God for His continued presence in Word and Sacrament. Seek opportunities to stay close to God as you study regularly His Word and receive the Lord's Supper.

Closing Worship

Sing or speak together the following stanzas of "God Himself Is Present."

God Himself is present;
Let us now adore Him
And with awe appear before Him.
God is in His temple;
All within keep silence,
Prostrate lie with deepest rev'rence.
Him alone God we own,
Him, our God and Savior;
Praise His name forever!

God Himself is present;
Hear the harps resounding;
See the hosts the throne surrounding!
"Holy, holy, holy!"
Hear the hymns ascending,
Songs of saints and angels blending.
Bow Your ear
To us hear:
Hear, O Christ, the praises
That Your Church now raises.

Adult Leaders Guide

Session 1

God Provides
a Leader for His People

(1 Samuel 16:1–23; 2 Samuel 1:1–6:23)

Focus

Theme: God Chooses!

Law/Gospel Focus

Invite a volunteer to read aloud the Law/Gospel Focus. Point out the Law found in the first two sentences and the Gospel found in the third sentence. Motivated by God's love for us in Christ Jesus we desire to respond. The response to the Gospel is found in the fourth sentence.

Objectives

Read aloud or invite volunteers to read aloud the objectives.

Opening Worship

Read in unison Psalm 24.

Introduction

Discuss the questions in this section. If your group is large, you may want to divide into smaller groups to allow each person to share. After small groups have discussed the questions, reassemble the large group to share answers.

1. Answers will vary. Some possible responses might include brave, honest, loving, and so on.

2. Often we look to outward appearances as we attempt to select a leader. Only God knows what is in the heart of an individual.

3. We seek God's guidance in selecting a leader so that the leader will affirm the Word of God, guide in a God-pleasing way, care for his/her people, and so on. We can pray to God for guidance as we select a leader.

Inform

Read aloud or invite volunteers to read aloud 1 Samuel 16:1–13. Then skim 2 Samuel 1:1–6:23.

About the Text

Invite volunteers to read aloud the commentary section. If time is short you may want to highlight specific points of information or interest.

Discussing the Text

1. God rejects Saul as leader because he has rejected God and His Word.

2. David has no particular apparent virtue that causes Samuel to choose him as Saul's successor. Instead, David is chosen king by the Lord's choice. God looks at David's heart and sees that he is, "A man after God's heart." Nothing we do can make us worthy of God's love. Only by God's grace—undeserved love—through faith are we made worthy.

3. The Lord sends Samuel to Bethlehem to anoint one of the sons of Jesse as the king. God has Samuel invite Jesse and his sons to the sacrifice. Each of the sons of Jesse pass in front of Samuel. Samuel thinks that the Lord will surely choose the eldest, Eliab, who is handsome and tall. The Lord rejects Eliab and tells Samuel that He does not judge by outward appearance. Jesse has seven sons pass before Samuel. The Lord does not choose any of them. Samuel asks Jesse, "Are these all the sons you have?" Jesse tells Samuel, "There is still the youngest." The Lord tells Samuel to anoint the youngest son, whose name is David. Samuel learns that the Lord's ways are not necessarily the ways of men.

4. Saul is jealous. On more than one occasion, Saul's jealousy rages and David's life is in jeopardy. God preserves David's life.

Connect

Read aloud the opening paragraphs. Then discuss the questions that follow.

1. Saul demonstrates contempt for God's Word. He seeks his own personal success and glory. People today ignore or disregard God's Word. In so doing they reject God. Many people today consider themselves number one. They seek their own personal success and glory, at times at the expense of others.

2. David is too young and a mere shepherd. In choosing David as king, God demonstrates His control in this world. Through this act God will equip His chosen people to serve Him. God often chooses the most unlikely people to serve Him. God rules through people.

3. As sinners we are separated from God and His love. In choosing us as His heirs, God demonstrates His boundless grace and mercy.

4. Answers will vary. Anytime we demonstrate love to others, do good works for others, and share Jesus' love with others we "declare the praises of Him."

Vision

To Do This Week

Urge participants to complete one or more of the Family Connection activities and one or both of the Personal Reflection activities during the coming week.

Closing Worship

Sing or speak together the stanzas of "Amazing Grace, How Sweet the Sound."

For Next Week

Urge participants to read 1 Samuel 17:55–20:42; 2 Samuel 5:1–5; 9:1–13; 11:1–12:13; 14:25–18:33; and 22:1–51 in preparation for the next session.

Session 2

God Preserves David

(1 Samuel 17:55–20:42; 2 Samuel 5:1–5; 9:1–13; 11:1–12:13; 14:25–18:33; 22:1–51)

Focus

Theme: Chosen, but Vulnerable

Invite volunteers to share what they believe the theme of this session means.

Law/Gospel Focus

Read aloud or invite a volunteer to read aloud the Law/Gospel Focus. Point out the Law found in the first and second sentences and the Gospel found in the second and third sentences.

Objectives

Invite volunteers to read aloud each of the objectives.

Opening Worship

Read in unison Psalm 23.

Introduction

Read aloud the opening paragraph. Then discuss the questions that follow. If the group is large, you may want to assign participants to smaller groups to discuss the questions. Then, after most groups have completed the questions, have everyone gather to hear the answers discussed in the small groups.

1. Christians are vulnerable to all kinds of temptations. In fact, Satan knows our personal weaknesses and will attack us at those points of weakness.

2. Allow time for participants to confess silently their sins.

3. Read aloud the words from 1 John 1:9 printed in the Study

Guide. God's Word assures us that as we confess our sins, God readily forgives those sins for Jesus' sake.

Read aloud the closing paragraph of this section. This paragraph serves as a bridge between the concept developed in the introduction and the concepts that will continue to be developed as the session proceeds.

Inform

Read aloud or invite volunteers to read aloud portions of the assigned Scripture passages. If time is short you may want to highlight the events found in the assigned passages.

About the Text

Read aloud the commentary or invite different volunteers to read aloud portions of it.

Discussing the Text

1. David faces adversities from his enemies and from his own sinful desires. Some of the adversities include Saul and his attempts to kill David, armies that seek to conquer Israel, and his own sexual desires.

2. Saul's attempts to kill David are prompted by jealousy and fear.

3. Jonathan tests Saul's intentions for David. David does not fellowship with the king. Instead, he excuses himself for the annual sacrificial meal of his kinsmen at Bethlehem. On the first day of David's plot, the king ignores David's absence. On the second day Saul's intentions are clearly revealed. When Jonathan excuses David on the ground that his duty to kinsmen takes precedence over that to the king, Saul breaks out in anger and disowns Jonathan, attempting to kill him. Jonathan now suffers affliction due to his love for David.

4. Jonathan is willing to give up his relationship to his father, peace in his family, and even his kingship because of his love for David.

5. God uses Jonathan's abiding friendship with David to preserve the future king's life.

Connect

Read aloud or invite volunteers to read aloud the opening paragraphs of this section. Then discuss the questions that follow.

1. David is a sinner as are you and I. The real hero in David's story is God Himself, who chooses to bless, forgives the sinful, and restores the ways of the righteous with His love.

2. Answers will vary.

3. Follow the directions indicated. Then have volunteers share their responses during the closing worship experience.

Vision

To Do This Week

Urge participants to complete one or more of the Family Connection and Personal Reflection activities during the coming week.

Closing Worship

Sing or speak together the stanzas of "Have No Fear, Little Flock" printed in the Study Guide. Then invite volunteers to share their additions to Martin Luther's words.

For Next Week

Urge participants to read 2 Samuel 9:1–13 in preparation for the next session.

David Shows Kindness to Mephibosheth

(2 Samuel 9:1–13)

Focus

Theme: In Response to God's Love

Ask, "What do we say and do in response to God's love for us?" Let volunteers respond.

Law/Gospel Focus

Read aloud or invite a volunteer to read aloud the Law/Gospel Focus. Ask participants to underline the Law statement once and the Gospel statement twice. The Law is found in the first sentence and the Gospel is found in the second. The third sentence includes a response to the Gospel message of love and forgiveness through faith in Christ Jesus. Point out that as sinners who have experienced the forgiveness Jesus won for us on the cross, it is natural for us to desire to demonstrate love for others.

Objectives

Read aloud or invite a different volunteer to read aloud each of the objectives.

Opening Worship

Read aloud in unison the confession of faith found in the words of Philippians 2:6–11.

Introduction

Read aloud the opening sentence. Then discuss the questions that follow. Again, if your group is large, you may want to assign participants to smaller groups to discuss the questions for this session. Bring the small groups together when most have finished answering the questions so that they can share their responses with the entire group.

1. Answers will vary. Kind words, caring gestures, and clear statements about our faith tell others that we are Christians.

2. Jesus tells us to love our enemies. Answers will vary.

3. While we were enemies of God, Jesus came into this world to suffer and to die for our sins.

4. Answers will vary. God's love for us in Christ Jesus empowers and motivates us to love others, even those who are most unlovable.

Read aloud the closing paragraph of this section.

Inform

Read aloud or invite a volunteer to read aloud 2 Samuel 9:1–13.

About the Text

Invite volunteers to read aloud portions of the commentary found in this section.

Discussing the Text

1. Saul and his sin brought much heartache and tragedy upon his own family.

2. Prompted by God's goodness to him, David seeks to show kindness to Saul's family.

3. David grants Mephibosheth all the crown land of his house and a personal invitation to live at the court. Mephibosheth will occupy a privileged status in David's royal court.

4. Mephibosheth's privileged status means that he will live and be treated like one of the king's sons.

Connect

Read aloud or invite volunteers to read aloud the opening paragraphs of this section. Then discuss the questions that follow.

1. Answers will vary. It will probably not be difficult for participants to discuss evidence of heartache and tragedy experienced in families today. Some heartaches and tragedies may include alcohol and drug abuse, physical and sexual abuse, divorce, marital unfaithfulness, and so forth. The root cause of all heartache is sin.

2. God's kindness is always rooted in His love for us in Christ. In His grace He sent His only Son Jesus into this world to suffer and to die on the cross for the sins of all people.

3. By God's grace through our faith in Christ Jesus, we have been made a royal people, a holy nation, a people belonging to Him. This privileged status means that we have the gift of eternal life with God in heaven. We are privileged to declare His praises to the world.

4. Answers will vary. Urge participants to include specific ways that they can demonstrate God's love in Christ to others.

Vision

To Do This Week

Urge participants to complete one or more of the Family Connection and Personal Reflection activities prior to the next time the group meets.

Closing Worship

Sing or speak together the first stanza of "Love Divine, All Love Excelling."

For Next Week

Urge participants to read 1 Kings 5:1–8:66 in preparation for the next session.

Session 4

Solomon Builds the Temple

(1 Kings 5:1–8:66)

Focus

Theme: House of Worship—Our Congregation

Law/Gospel Focus

Read aloud or invite a volunteer to read aloud the Law/Gospel Focus. Have participants underline once the sentence containing the Law and twice the sentence containing the Gospel. The Law is found in the first sentence and the Gospel is found in the second and third sentences.

Objectives

Read aloud or invite a different volunteer to read aloud each of the objectives.

Opening Worship

Read in unison Psalm 119:105–112.

Introduction

Read aloud the introductory paragraph. Then have a different volunteer read aloud the two advertisements.

1. The first advertisement focuses on the building and its furnishings. The second advertisement focuses on what happens to and between people inside the church building.

2. The second advertisement best describes a Scriptural understanding of the church.

3. People do not like to consider their sins. Many churches today have tried to accommodate people's aversion to the concept of sin by focusing on the good inside all people. Scripture teaches that all people have sinned and therefore face eternal damnation.

A congregation that ignores or disregards the Law has little need for sharing the Gospel. The true church also shares God's love and forgiveness in Jesus Christ.

Read aloud the closing paragraph of this section.

Inform

Read aloud or invite volunteers to read aloud 1 Kings 5:1–8:66.

About the Text

Invite volunteers to read aloud portions of this commentary.

Discussing the Text

Discuss the questions in this section.

1. The temple is the central place for the people of God to gather to offer sacrifices and worship Him.

2. Only after God approves does work on the temple begin. God is also involved in directing the dedication activities.

3. God and His presence are clearly the focus of the dedication of the temple. This is significant because after building such a magnificent structure, people might have attempted to take credit for the temple. Instead, God remains the focus in the dedication. The temple is God's, built under His guidance and direction.

Connect

Read aloud or invite volunteers to read aloud this section. Then discuss the questions that follow.

1. What happens inside a church is more important than what the church looks like. The most important things that can occur within a church are that God's Word is taught in truth and purity and His sacraments are administered according to His Word.

2. Jesus came not as a cloud but in human flesh. Jesus is the true temple of God, the Lord who came to His own and took upon Himself the sins of all people.

3. God remains present for His people today in Word and Sacrament. Again, the Christian church is the place where the Word of God is taught in truth and purity and the sacraments are administered according to God's Word.

Vision

To Do This Week

Urge participants to complete one or more of the suggested Family Connection and Personal Reflection activities.

Closing Worship

Sing or speak together the first two stanzas of "God Himself Is Present."

For Next Week

Urge participants to read 1 Kings 17:1–19:18 and 2 Kings 1:1–2:18 in preparation for the next session.

Session 5

Elijah Goes to Heaven

(1 Kings 17:1–19:18; 2 Kings 1:1–2:18)

Focus

Theme: Hope in the Midst of Hardship

Read aloud the theme. Then ask, "Who has experienced hope in the midst of hardship? How?"

Law/Gospel Focus

Read aloud or invite a volunteer to read aloud the Law/Gospel Focus. Ask participants to underline once the sentence containing the Law and twice the sentence containing the Gospel. The Law is found in the first two sentences and the Gospel is found in the third.

Objectives

Invite a different volunteer to read aloud each of the objectives.

Opening Worship

Sing or speak together the stanzas of "Have No Fear, Little Flock."

Introduction

1. Answers will vary. Invite volunteers to share. Don't force anyone to share who may feel uncomfortable doing so.

2. Answers will vary. Don't expect that everyone dealt with a hardship in the same—or even an appropriate—way.

3. A hardship can cause a person to ask God, "Why me?" or "Where were you?"

4. People facing a hardship may realize that they are helpless on their own to deal with the challenges life may bring. They fall on

129

their knees, realizing that only God can help them through the hardship.

5. Jesus invites all who are weary and burdened to come to Him. He promises to give us rest.

Read aloud the closing paragraph of this section.

Inform

Invite volunteers to read aloud 1 Kings 17:1–19:18 and 2 Kings 1:1–2:18.

About the Text

Read aloud portions of the commentary and then invite volunteers to read aloud other portions.

Discussing the Text

1. Elijah confronts the kings with their sins so that they might repent of their sins and return to the one true God. Elijah announces God's punishment upon the land.

2. Elijah speaks and acts on the authority of God and supplies flour and oil for the widow of Zarephath and her family during the famine. Later, Elijah brings the dead son of the widow back to life.

3. King Ahaziah sends messengers to Baal to see if he will recover from his injuries. The messengers are confronted by Elijah. Each of the companies of soldiers the king sends to Elijah is consumed by fire. Ahaziah dies of his injuries.

4. Elijah is taken into heaven accompanied by a fiery chariot and horses or described as such. This miraculous event serves as a sign to Elisha that he is to replace Elijah.

Connect

Read aloud or invite volunteers to read aloud the opening paragraphs of this section. Then discuss the questions that follow.

1. God is concerned about not only our spiritual but also our physical and emotional well-being.

2. Because of our sin, we too deserve to die, since the wages of sin is death.

3. Jesus' death and resurrection are the remedy for sin and eternal separation from God. Through Christ, God redeemed the world from the curse of the Law and from idolatry and rebellion.

4. God is with us always. God is with us during the good times and the bad times. The Spirit of God guides and supports us as we seek to follow Jesus and serve His people in this world.

Vision

To Do This Week

Urge participants to complete one or more of the suggested Family Connection and Personal Reflection activities prior to the next time the group meets.

Closing Worship

Sing or speak together the first stanza of "On Christ's Ascension I Now Build."

For Next Week

Urge participants to read 2 Kings 5:1–19 in preparation for the next session.

Session 6

God Heals Naaman

(2 Kings 5:1–19)

Focus

Theme: God's Ways vs. Human Expectations

Ask, "How are God's ways sometimes different than human expectations?" Allow time for a few participants to respond. Then move into the session.

Law/Gospel Focus

Read aloud the Law/Gospel Focus. Have volunteers identify the sentences containing the Law and the Gospel. The Law is found in the first sentence and the Gospel is found in the second, third, fourth, and fifth sentences.

Objectives

Invite a different volunteer to read aloud each of the objectives.

Opening Worship

Read in unison Psalm 119:161–168.

Introduction

Read aloud the opening paragraph. Then have a different volunteer read aloud each of the statements. Read aloud the closing sentence. Then discuss the questions that follow.

1. The people face eternal death. They are relying upon themselves for their salvation.

2. Answers will vary. Because of sin, people often look in all the wrong places to find the salvation that Jesus won for them on the cross. The fact remains that no eternal life exists apart from faith in Christ Jesus.

3. Answers will vary. We can share with others the reason for the certainty we have about our eternal destiny; that is, Jesus Christ crucified.

Read aloud the closing paragraph.

Inform

Read aloud or invite a volunteer to read aloud 2 Kings 5:1–19.

About the Text

Invite volunteers to read aloud the commentary.

Discussing the Text

1. Naaman is commander of the Aramean army. The dark cloud of leprosy hangs over his life.

2. The young Israelite girl taken as a slave by a raiding party becomes God's chosen instrument. She testifies to the living God.

3. Naaman cannot and does not understand how washing in the Jordan River will heal him.

4. The purpose of Elisha's prescription for healing calls forth faith. Naaman will be healed by the power of God not Elisha.

5. Naaman's new faith finds expression in his desire to sacrifice to God, even when he returns to his native Aram. From now on, Naaman will serve the one true God.

Connect

Read aloud or invite a volunteer to read aloud this section. Then discuss the questions that follow.

1. Naaman demands signs and wonders, impressive displays of authority. Instead, God uses simple means to wash away the disease afflicting Naaman.

2. Jesus' death on the cross brings us full healing, healing that will last into eternity—forgiveness of sins and a body untouched by disease or even death in eternal life.

3. In the waters of Holy Baptism we have been washed clean of our sin and made to be a new creation.

4. Today, God continues to work through simple means to provide healing and strength to sinners. The Lord works through

water and His Word in Holy Baptism to bring us into a covenant relationship with Him. God also works through simple bread and wine in which He provides the body and blood of His own dear Son. Through the Lord's Supper, God grants us forgiveness of sins and the strengthening of our faith.

Vision

To Do This Week

Urge participants to complete one or more of the suggested Family Connection and Personal Reflection activities prior to the next time the group meets.

Closing Worship

Pray together the prayer adapted from the Order of Holy Baptism.

For Next Week

Urge participants to read 2 Kings 11:1–12:21 in preparation for the next session.

Session 7

Joash Rules Judah

(2 Kings 11:1–12:21)

Focus

Theme: God in Control!

Law/Gospel Focus

Read aloud the Law/Gospel Focus. Have participants underline once the sentence containing the Law and twice the sentence containing the Gospel. The Law is found in the first sentence and the Gospel is found in the second and third sentences.

Opening Worship

Sing or speak together the stanzas of "Lord, Take My Hand and Lead Me" printed in the Study Guide.

Introduction

Ask the question, "Who's in charge here?" Then discuss the questions that follow.

1. Answers will vary. Often when disagreements arise or chaos emerges, the questions may be asked.

2. Answers will vary. Allow time for participants to share.

3. Answers will vary. Keep in mind that for some individuals experiencing hardships now, God may not have visible control at this time.

Read aloud the closing paragraph of this section.

Inform

Read aloud or invite volunteers to read aloud portions of the assigned Scripture passages.

About the Text

Have volunteers read aloud portions of the commentary.

Discussing the Text

1. God demonstrates His control by providing an escape for Joash through his aunt, Jehosheba. Jehosheba hides Joash for six years in the priestly quarters of the temple.

2. Athaliah wants the boy killed so that he cannot be crowned ruler. It would take careful steps to overthrow the wicked queen.

3. Joash and the nation renew their covenant relationship and pledge to observe the Lord's commands and decrees. Joash restores the worship of the true God and destroys the temple, idols, and priests of Baal. Joash also works to restore the temple of the Lord, and asks about it later.

4. Joash becomes tolerant of Baal worship and even kills Zechariah, Jehoiada's son. When Jerusalem is threatened by Hazael, king of Aram, Joash does not trust in God but buys his and the city's freedom by giving as a ransom the sacred vessels, furnishings, and substantial funds from the temple.

Connect

Read aloud the opening paragraphs of this section. Then discuss the questions that follow.

1. Wickedness and ruin follow when people no longer listen to or follow God's Word. The same occurs today.

2. God orchestrates the hiding of Joash so that he will not be put to death. God preserves the line of David with a man who renewed worship, preparing for the Messiah. Answers will vary. Allow time for volunteers to share.

3. Answers will vary. As our heavenly Father greets us in heaven, we will see that Jesus has walked with us, guiding and protecting us and working His plan for our good.

Vision

To Do This Week

Urge participants to complete one or more of the suggested Family Connection and Personal Reflection activities prior to the next group session.

Closing Worship

Speak together in unison Psalm 119:105–112.

For Next Week

Urge participants to read Jonah 1:1–4:11 in preparation for the next session.

Session 8

Jonah Preaches God's Word in Nineveh

(Jonah 1:1–4:11)

Focus

Theme: No Limit to God's Grace

Law/Gospel Focus

Read aloud or invite a volunteer to read aloud the Law/Gospel Focus. Have participants underline once the sentences containing the Law and twice the sentences containing the Gospel. The Law is found in the first two sentences and the Gospel is found in the third and fourth sentences.

Objectives

Have a different volunteer read aloud each of the objectives.

Opening Worship

Pray together the prayer for steadfast faith.

Introduction

Read aloud the opening quotations. Then discuss the questions that follow.

1. Answers will vary. Seeking only "good" members could certainly limit God's grace. Moving to a new location might help to attract some new members, but it might also limit the grace God will share with the new community where the congregation is currently located. The third quote limits God's grace to individuals who have not experienced divorce.

2. Answers will vary.

3. Answers will vary. The statement "No limit to God's grace" indicates that a congregation seeks new ways to reach out into the community sharing the Gospel of Jesus Christ.

Read aloud the closing paragraph of this section.

Inform

Read aloud or invite volunteers to read aloud portions of Jonah 1:1–4:11.

About the Text

Invite different volunteers to read portions of the commentary.

Discussing the Text

1. What may have begun as fear and intimidation is disclosed at the end of the account as Jonah's attempt to limit God's grace to his own nation.

2. Jonah plans to travel from Joppa in the opposite direction, to Tarshish, to avoid God's mission.

3. God determines the course and events of history. He controls the forces of nature and works in spite of Jonah's rebellion and disobedience. When lots are cast to discern God's will during the storm, Jonah acknowledges his guilt before God. The crew casts Jonah overboard. The storm stops as quickly as it started. A "great fish" swallows Jonah as the means by which God will preserve His servant for the mission to Nineveh.

4. Jonah admits his guilt before the crew and before God.

5. By the power of the Holy Spirit working through God's Word coming from Jonah's mouth, Jonah's mission to Nineveh is successful. The people of Nineveh believe God, repent of their sins, and call upon God to be merciful and forgive their sins.

6. Jonah complains to the Lord because he desires the Lord's blessing to apply only to the people of Israel. God demonstrates His love for all people by forgiving and blessing the people of Nineveh.

Connect

Read aloud the opening paragraphs of this section or invite a volunteer to do so. Then discuss the questions that follow.

1. God speaks Law to confront and humble sinful human beings. God speaks His Law "so that every mouth may be silenced, and the whole world may be held accountable" (Romans 3:19). No one can earn, barter for, or buy salvation through the Law.

2. Jonah shares the love and forgiveness of God. The prophets of the Old Testament share the task of announcing the world's redeemer promised to Israel and revealed in the person and work of Jesus Christ. God reminds people of His grace in the Word and Sacrament ministry of the local church and the mission proclamation of Christ, and people are brought to faith by the power of the Holy Spirit working through the Gospel.

3. Answers will vary. God continues to strengthen the faith of believers, enabling them to share His Good News of forgiveness of sins and eternal life through Christ with family, friends, loved ones, strangers, and so on. God lets His light shine in us, often first through good deeds, then through a literal message of Law and Gospel, so that others may praise His holy name.

Vision

To Do This Week

Urge participants to complete one or more of the suggested Family Connection activities and the Personal Reflection activities prior to the next time the group meets.

Closing Worship

Sing or speak together the stanzas of "Love in Christ Is Strong and Living" found in the Study Guide.

For Next Week

Urge participants to read Isaiah 6:1–8; 9:1–6; 2 Kings 4:8–17 in preparation for the next session.

God Calls Isaiah

(Isaiah 6:1–8; 9:1–6; 2 Kings 4:8–17)

Focus

Theme: The Lord Saves

Law/Gospel Focus

Read aloud or invite a volunteer to read aloud the Law/Gospel Focus. Ask participants to identify the sentences containing the Law and the sentences containing the Gospel. The Law is found in the first two sentences. The Gospel is found in the third, fourth, and fifth sentences.

Objectives

Invite a different volunteer to read aloud each of the objectives.

Opening Worship

Sing or speak together "Isaiah, Mighty Seer, in Spirit Soared."

Introduction

Discuss each of the questions found in the introduction.

1. Answers will vary. Some parents give their children names based on the names of grandparents, parents, or friends. Other parents may give their children names based upon biblical events.

2. Answers will vary.

3. Answers will vary. Isaiah's name is a message of Gospel to a people who had turned away from God. The name Isaiah reveals, the kind of message he will share, and the purpose for his ministry. It is likely that participants know little about the life and ministry of Isaiah.

Inform

Read aloud or invite volunteers to read aloud Isaiah 6:1–8 and 9:1–6.

About the Text

Invite different volunteers to read aloud portions of the commentary.

Discussing the Text

1. "The Lord saves" is part of the message that Isaiah proclaims to an erring nation.

2. Isaiah sees and describes the heavenly scene in vivid language and imagery. He sees supernatural beings, seraphs, who worship before the throne of God. The chorus of angels cries, "Holy, holy, holy," testifying to the triune nature of the living God. He is called to be a spokesman of God's message to His fallen people.

3. Isaiah responds to the vision in humility and awe. Isaiah confesses that he is lost and condemned and stands completely at the mercy of the almighty God.

4. In love God reaches out through the seraph's tong and the hot coal to remove the prophet's sin. Isaiah is redeemed from sin and renewed and strengthened for the tasks of his ministry. Isaiah is ready by God's grace to respond, "Here am I. Send me!"

5. Isaiah speaks both God's Law and His Gospel. Isaiah's prophecy of the royal Son, who reigns on the throne of David, illustrates God's promise for a glorious future.

Connect

Read aloud or invite volunteers to read aloud the opening paragraphs of this section. Then discuss the questions that follow.

1. Isaiah is an inadequate sinner, separated from God by his sin. God gives Isaiah a glimpse into heaven and commissions him for ministry. God continues to reach out to sinners today through the Gospel. We deserve nothing but condemnation. But by grace

through faith in Jesus' death on the cross, we receive the forgiveness of sins and eternal life. God's love for us empowers and motivates us to serve Him.

2. God continues to confront people with His holiness and reveals the depths of human depravity. No person has sufficient strength or merit to stand before God. God provides grace in the full Word and Sacrament ministry. Through faith in Jesus' death and resurrection, believers have full access to God's love and forgiveness.

3. Through faith strengthened by the power of the Holy Spirit working through God's Word and Sacraments, we are empowered to share His Law and His Gospel with people today.

Vision

To Do This Week

Urge participants to complete one or more of the suggested Family Connection activities and one or both of the Personal Reflection activities prior to the next time the group meets.

Closing Worship

Pray together the prayer printed in the Study Guide.

For Next Week

Urge participants to read 2 Kings 18:1–20:11 in preparation for the next session.

Session 10

Hezekiah Prays to God

(2 Kings 18:1–20:11)

Focus

Theme: Comfort and Hope in Times of Crisis

Law/Gospel Focus

Read aloud or invite a volunteer to read aloud the Law/ Gospel Focus. Point out the Law found in the first sentence and the Gospel found in the second, third, and fourth sentences.

Objectives

Invite a different volunteer to read aloud each of the objectives.

Opening Worship

Sing or speak together "I Walk in Danger All the Way."

Introduction

1. Have participants review the dangers mentioned in the hymn. Answers about the dangers participants have faced or are facing will vary.

2. Responses will vary.

3. Read together Psalm 23. God is with us always, even as we face dangers, hardships, and crises—even as we go through the Valley of the Shadow of Death.

Inform

Read aloud 2 Kings 18:1–20:11. If time is short, you may want to preselect sections of the Scripture passages to read and summarize the events that occur in the passages not read.

About the Text

Read aloud or invite volunteers to read aloud portions of the commentary.

Discussing the Text

1. The name Hezekiah means "Yahweh strengthens." Hezekiah's name reveals the fact that he relies on the Word of the Lord for faith-strengthening power and as the source of his conviction and integrity.

2. Under Hezekiah's leadership, the doors of the Lord's temple are again opened and the priests remove the idols from the sanctuary and sanctify God's house for public worship. Hezekiah calls the nation to repentance and genuine faith in the living God. He also reinitiates the Passover celebration.

3. Hezekiah struggles with the sin of pride, which leads him to depend upon himself rather than on God.

4. Hezekiah's faith is tested when Judah is invaded by King Sennacherib of Assyria. Through God strengthening Hezekiah's faith-led leadership, the people maintain their confidence in Hezekiah and their faith in the Lord. The Lord triumphs.

5. The shadow retreats 10 steps, moving suddenly backwards on the stairway of Ahaz as a sign of God's healing.

Connect

Invite volunteers to read aloud portions of this section. Then discuss the questions that follow.

1. Although Hezekiah and his nation are threatened with annihilation, God saves them. Answers will vary. God alone has the power to save. God acts powerfully in your life to bring you to the one true faith by the power of the Holy Spirit working through the Gospel, even if we are threatened with difficulties and dangers.

2. The Law discloses the universal human condition of sin. The Gospel proclaims that God has acted to save His people. Through Christ, God has conquered the enemy and won the battle for eternal life for all people.

3. The victory that Hezekiah experiences by God's grace is the final victory for all God's people—the victory of salvation in Christ Jesus.

4. Under Christ's protective care, we can endure temptations and trouble because we know that our Lord and Savior walks with us always.

Vision

To Do This Week

Urge participants to complete one or more of the suggested Family Connection activities and the Personal Reflection activities prior to the next time the group meets.

Closing Worship

Sing or speak together the stanzas of "Jesus Sinners Will Receive" printed in the Study Guide.

For Next Week

Urge participants to read Jeremiah 1:1–19; 7:1–29; 18:1–12; 19:1–15; 20:1–6; 23:5–6; 28:1–17; 31:31–34; 37:1–39:18; and 2 Chronicles 20:1–30 in preparation for the next session.

Session 11

God Works through Jeremiah and Jehoshaphat

(Jeremiah 1:1–19; 7:1–29; 18:1–12; 19:1–15; 20:1–6; 23:5–6; 28:1–17; 31:31–34; 37:1–39:18; 2 Chronicles 20:1–30)

Focus

Theme: Ready to Forgive

Law/Gospel Focus

Read aloud or invite a volunteer to read aloud the Law/Gospel Focus. Ask the participants to identify the Law and the Gospel. Point out that the Law is found in the first sentence and the Gospel is found in the last three sentences.

Objectives

Read aloud the objectives.

Opening Worship

Sing or speak the first stanza of "The Law of God Is Good and Wise" and the first stanza of "The Gospel Shows the Father's Grace."

Introduction

1. Encourage participants to provide endings to the statement "I'm ready to ..." in as many different ways as possible. Answers will vary.

2. Answers will vary.

3. God continues to invite sinners to Him. He calls people to repent of their sin so that they might receive His forgiveness and the gift of eternal life. Ultimately, rejecting God's forgiveness will

mean eternal damnation. Thankfully, God often offers His grace time and again.

Read aloud the closing paragraph of this section.

Inform

Skim Jeremiah 1:1–19; 7:1–29; 18:1–12; 19:1–15; 20:1–6; 23:5–6; 28:1–17; 31:31–34; 37:1–39:18; and 2 Chronicles 20:1–30.

About the Text

Invite volunteers to read aloud the commentary. If time is short you may wish to summarize the important information included in the commentary.

Discussing the Text

1. Jeremiah prophesies under five kings, of whom only one is described as God-fearing. Some threatened his life. Jeremiah also faces opposition from false prophets and is a frequent target of ridicule and persecution for his faithfulness to God's Word. God was always with him.

2. God calls Jeremiah to service and provides him the strength and skill for ministry. The branch of an almond tree and a large boiling kettle confirm Jeremiah's call. Both of these images reveal the nature of Jeremiah's ministry.

3. The people continue to ignore Jeremiah's message and tragically continue to follow the false prophets. The consequence for their rebellion against God is that their nation is punished.

4. God promises to make a new covenant (31:31–34), rooted not in the people's commitment, but upon His love and mercy.

5. King Jehoshaphat not only abolishes idolatry, but introduces a national reform, dispatching officials, Levites, and the priests throughout Judah to teach the people "the Book of the Law."

6. Jehoshaphat admits the nation's utter helplessness and total dependence on God for a military victory. The Lord confuses the enemy soldiers so that they destroy one another. The Lord's army does not have to strike one blow. Jehoshaphat responds in praise and thanksgiving for God's deliverence.

Connect

Read aloud or invite volunteers to read aloud the paragraphs in this section. Then discuss the questions that follow.

1. The goal of Jeremiah's preaching is to call people to repentance so that they might receive God's forgiveness. Today, faithful pastors continue to preach God's Law so that people realize the depravity of their sins and need for a Savior. Jeremiah shares with the people God's eagerness to forgive them. Pastors today share the message of God's Word, including His offer of forgiveness for all people, won through Jesus' death on the cross.

2. People today often reject the message of the forgiveness and eternal life Jesus won for them on the cross.

3. A small number of God's Old Testament people heard the message, implored God's forgiveness, and believed His promise to redeem His chosen people. In Jesus Christ, God fulfilled His promises and instituted a new covenant in His Son's death and resurrection. We receive the forgiveness of sins and the gift of eternal life by God's grace through faith in Christ Jesus.

Vision

To Do This Week

Urge participants to do one or both of the suggested Family Connection activities and one or more of the suggested Personal Reflection activities prior to the next time the group meets.

Closing Worship

Pray together the prayer for steadfast faith printed in the Study Guide.

For Next Week

Urge participants to read Daniel 3:1–30 in preparation for the next session.

Session 12

God Saves Daniel's Three Friends

(Daniel 3:1–30)

Focus

Theme: Who Is Your God?

Ask participants to consider the question "Who is your God?" Ask, "How would you answer someone who asked you that question?" Allow time for volunteers to respond.

Law/Gospel Focus

Read aloud or invite a volunteer to read aloud the Law/Gospel Focus. Have participants underline once the sentence containing the Law and twice the sentences containing the Gospel. The Law is found in the first sentence. The Gospel is found in the second, third, and fourth sentences.

Objectives

Invite a different volunteer to read aloud each of the objectives for this session.

Opening Worship

Speak in unison the words of the Apostles' Creed.

Introduction

Read aloud the opening paragraph. Then discuss the questions that follow.

1. Answers will vary. Christians often confess gods of materialism, power, pride, jealousy, sex, alcohol, and so on with their words and actions.

2. Anything that becomes number one in your life other than the one true God will crowd God out of your life. God tells us in His Word, "You cannot serve two masters."

3. Although we are sinners, God sent His only Son, Jesus, to earth to suffer and die for our sins.

Read aloud the closing paragraph of this section.

Inform

Read Daniel 3:1–30.

About the Text

Read aloud or invite volunteers to read aloud portions of the commentary.

Discussing the Text

1. Each story in the book of Daniel takes place in the sixth century B.C. in Babylon. God's people face persecution and hardships in a pagan nation, but God comforts His people, protecting them from harm.

2. Nebuchadnezzar is furious with the youths' refusal to worship the golden image. It was an issue of pride and wilful defiance.

3. Shadrach, Meshach, and Abednego demonstrate faith and obedience to God by refusing to bow down to the image and by resolving to obey God.

4. Nebuchadnezzar orders the three young men to burn to death in a fiery furnace made even hotter for the crime.

5. God controls the fate of His servants. The "son of the gods" in the furnace is the Lord's messenger, an angel sent to defend and preserve Shadrach, Meshach, and Abednego from the destruction that would certainly occur in the fiery furnace. Nebuchadnezzar responds to God's mighty act of deliverance by affirming God's power.

Connect

Read aloud or invite a volunteer to read aloud the commentary. Then discuss the questions that follow.

1. God works to extend His saving Word and purpose throughout the country through the young men. God has chosen us by His

grace through faith to extend His saving Word and purpose in our homes, in our communities, in our nation, and in our world.

2. We at times can face persecution or rejection by obeying God's Law. God's Law is at times very unpopular (e.g., regarding the abortion issue, honesty and integrity, and euthanasia) or even rejected by society. Answers will vary.

3. Materialism, sex, ambition, and power are just a few of the gods of personal success and fulfillment before which people bow down.

4. God declares us "not guilty" because the Savior of the world has taken upon Himself the punishment we deserve. God's Son walked into the fiery furnace of death to save us from eternal judgment.

Vision

To Do This Week

Urge participants to complete one or more of the suggested Family Connection activities and one or more of the suggested Personal Reflection activities prior to the next time the group meets.

Closing Worship

Sing or speak together the stanza of "I Walk in Danger All the Way" printed in the Study Guide.

For Next Week

Urge participants to read 2 Chronicles 36:5–23; Psalm 137:1–4; and Daniel 6:1–28 and 9:1–19 in preparation for the next session.

Session 13

God Keeps His People Safe

(2 Chronicles 36:5–23; Psalm 137:1–4;
Daniel 6:1–28; 9:1–19)

Focus

Theme: The Price of Faith

Ask participants, "What is the cost of salvation?" Allow time for volunteers to respond. Say, "In today's session we will learn the cost of salvation."

Law/Gospel Focus

Read aloud or invite a volunteer to read aloud the Law/Gospel Focus. Point out the Law found in the first sentence and the Gospel found in the second and third sentences.

Objectives

Invite a different volunteer to read aloud each of the objectives for this session.

Opening Worship

Speak in unison the words of Paul found in Philippians 2:5–11.

Introduction

Discuss the questions.

1. Answers will vary.

2. Answers will vary. Encourage participants to share openly and honestly.

3. Answers will vary. We may have to face rejection or persecution if we share our faith in Jesus.

Read aloud the closing paragraph of this section.

Inform

Read aloud or invite volunteers to read aloud portions of 2 Chronicles 36:5–23; Psalm 137:1–4; and Daniel 6:1–28 and 9:1–19. If time is short, you may wish to limit your reading to the Scripture passages from Daniel.

About the Text

Read aloud or invite volunteers to read aloud the commentary.

Discussing the Text

1. Darius's plan to make Daniel the senior administrator causes the other officials to become jealous. The other officials discredit his service to the king by attacking his ultimate loyalty. Daniel's faith in God will not allow him to worship an idol or mere human being. The king's decree to bow down and worship him becomes the pretext to accuse Daniel of treason.

2. The king's decree to bow down and worship him becomes the pretext for the officials to accuse Daniel of treason. Darius, grieved by the verdict against his loyal servant, asks God's blessing upon Daniel in the face of certain death.

3. God closes the mouths of the beasts to rescue His prophet from the den of the lions. Darius releases Daniel from the sentence of death and takes revenge upon the instigators of the trouble.

4. Like Nebuchadnezzar, Darius is a polytheist who views his kingdom as the most powerful of nations. His letter to the nations acknowledges that God is worthy of praise and respect, but falls short of acknowledging God as the only true God.

Connect

Read aloud or invite volunteers to read aloud the opening paragraphs of this section. Then discuss the questions that follow.

1. We at times worship wealth, power, prestige, alcohol and drugs, sex, tradition, and so on. These all evidence the fact that people today continue to worship the created rather than the Creator.

2. Despite our sin, God is our gracious Savior through the blood of Jesus Christ shed on the cross. In Jesus' death and resurrection we are washed clean and raised from the death of sin to live a new life.

3. Jesus remains present with us today in Word and Sacrament. Through these means Jesus forgives our sins and strengthens our faith for service to Him. Through faith in Christ Jesus, we can stand firm and resist the lures and temptations of this hostile world. We can trust His mighty power to save.

Vision

To Do This Week

Urge participants to complete one or more of the suggested Family Connection activities and one or both of the Personal Reflection activities.

Closing Worship

Sing or speak together the stanzas of "God Himself Is Present" printed in the Study Guide.